Praise for
Customer CEO and **Chuck Wall**

"I've felt for a long time that satisfied customers are not enough. What you need are customers who are so pleased by the way you treat them that they want to brag about you. They become part of your sales force. If you want to create those kinds of Raving Fan customers, read *Customer CEO* and let Chuck Wall guide your journey."
—Ken Blanchard, coauthor of
The One Minute Manager® and *Raving Fans*

"For years I've been teaching brands how to fascinate their customers. What I love about Chuck Wall's approach is how vividly he illustrates that customer holds equal, if not more, power than brands. Today, marketers don't lead the message—the market does. In this fascinating book, Chuck Wall teaches how."
—Sally Hogshead, Hall of Fame speaker and author of
FASCINATE: Your 7 Triggers to Persuade and Captivate

"The 21st century's free market capitalism obsession with maximizing shareholder value has one major flaw: the most important enterprise stake holder, the customer, does not have a seat at the table. Chuck Wall's brilliant *Customer CEO* articulates why tomorrow's successful companies must insist on the shareholders' need to share the spotlight with a business's prime constituency—the customer."
—Peter Georgescu, chairman emeritus, Young & Rubicam

"*Customer CEO* provides great vision on what truly matters in the rapidly changing world of servicing customers. Culture in an organization is strongest when there is a clear vision and a consistent message. *Customer CEO* is the tool needed to get everyone in your organization moving in the same direction. Chuck's examples of successes and failures provide up-to-date insight into how to recognize the power of your customers. If your business has customers, everyone in your organization, from the C-suite to the frontline, should read this book!"
—Chris Zane, founder and president Zane's Cycles,
author of *Reinventing the Wheel: The Science of
Creating Lifetime Customers*

"Wow, talk about 'voice of the customer!' Chuck Wall has come face-to-face with more than 100,000 customers in his 30-year career, along the way collecting many inspiring stories and terrific examples of great service. *Customer CEO* is not just entertaining, but well worth the read, no matter what part of the business you're in."

—Don Peppers and Martha Rogers, PhD, authors of
Extreme Trust: Honesty as a Competitive Advantage

"Chuck Wall has been designing a better future for his clients for a long time by teaching them the importance of first designing a better future for their own customers. *Customer CEO* shows every size and type of organization the best path to take to profit from the power of their customers. This will be a book that will change forever the way you think about your customers."

—Tom Cuthbert, Vistage Chair

"In *Customer CEO*, Chuck Wall does much more than confront and overturn longstanding but obsolete marketing strategies. He literally gives today's customer a voice and lays out a roadmap for exactly how you must listen, act, and partner as a brand to profit in a market where power, persuasion, and media are shared with consumers." —Simon Mainwaring, founder and CEO, WeFirst

"The internet and social media have given customers a voice as important and strong as the companies serving them. Chuck Wall showcases dozens of companies that have succeeded by putting their customers first. In *Customer CEO*, Chuck will focus—or refocus you—on the voice of your customers. Let him lead you through the steps you need to follow to create a lasting enterprise."

—Morris Miller, CEO of Xenex Healthcare
Services and cofounder of Rackspace

"Most of us hope to to succeed in one business. Chuck Wall is a master entrepreneur who has succeeded in many businesses. He succeeds because regardless of his business, he's understood his customers and treated them like they were in charge. Chuck understands that the customer is CEO and what business owners need to do about it. You'll like the wisdom he shares in this book."

—Brad Aronson, entrepreneur and investor

CUSTOMER

CEO

How to Profit from the Power of Your Customers

CHUCK WALL

bibliomotion
books + media

First published by Bibliomotion, Inc.

33 Manchester Road
Brookline, MA 02446
Tel: 617-934-2427
www.bibliomotion.com

Customer CEO™, Profit from the Power of Your Customers™, and Customer Thinking™ are trademarks of Charles B. Wall.

Printed in the United States of America

Library of Congress Cataloging-in-Publication Data

Wall, Chuck.
    Customer CEO : how to profit from the power of your customers / Chuck Wall.
        pages cm
    Includes bibliographical references and index.
    ISBN 978-1-937134-37-2 (hardcover : alk. paper)—
ISBN 978-1-937134-38-9 (ebook)— ISBN 978-1-937134-39-6
(enhanced ebook)
    1. Customer services.   2. Customer relations.   I. Title.
    HF5415.5.W343 2013
    658.8'12—dc23
                    2012047158

To Franze, Martha, Chuck, and Alex. All my love and gratitude for keeping me humble and focused on what truly matters more than myself.

FOREWORD

If you are in business today it's not news that every customer is more demanding than ever before. They expect perfection and can be utterly brutal in their assessment of your performance. Between texting, tweeting, and talking to their tribes of friends and followers they can create utter chaos.

The question is what are you going to do about it?

I believe Chuck Wall couldn't have written his first book, *Customer CEO*, at a more opportune time. Chuck is a successful entrepreneur, having started seven different companies in several different industries. He is an expert marketer who has never been satisfied with the status quo; he recognized he had to find innovative ways to differentiate his own enterprises as well as the clients he has helped during his career. That's why he became an expert at what is now called Big Data; using business intelligence analytics to understand *what* people did. But, Chuck recognized that reams of data were just a small part of the equation. The secret to successfully acquiring and retaining customers in this hypercompetitive world is to also intimately understand customer goals, frustrations, and obstacles in life. It's not enough to just add a few new features or services to your business offerings. The central question is how to help people accomplish the jobs that will improve their lives. To discover this, Chuck began interviewing and surveying customers from every walk of life. He's listened to well over 100,000 of them in order to climb inside their heads to understand their *why*. His primary research has shown him that customer's possess nine powers that you must actively engage if you want to win their minds, hearts, and wallets.

Customer CEO is a perfect metaphor for today's customer. Businesses used to be in control and could dictate terms, price, and features in the transaction. But, now transactions have given way to relationships and the customer is in charge. Social media means having 24/7 relationships whether you want them or not. *Customer CEO* is stuffed full of real-life business stories from dozens of companies that understand this new reality. Chuck's stories will instruct and inspire you, no matter what size your company. There is practical advice on every page.

Chuck ties it all together with his unique method of linking Big Data and customer insight. This is what he calls *Customer Thinking*. He lays out a straightforward way for every company to do the work that will allow them to profitably grow by truly understanding their customers. Instead of being adversaries, the book shows you how to build long-lasting relationships with them. *Customer CEO* is truly your secret weapon to show you how to do exactly that: profit from the power of your customers.

Finally, Chuck has a real passion for people. I am particularly pleased to see that he is engaging you the reader directly through what he calls the *Power of Purpose* by donating a portion of the proceeds for every copy of *Customer CEO* to support the worthwhile mission of *Compassion's Water of Life* efforts to provide a lifetime's worth of clean water to a family in the developing world.

Customer CEO provides you with many of the answers you've long been searching for. I believe it will transform both you and your customers for good.

Michael Port

AUTHOR'S NOTE

I know you could have selected many other fine business books to read so I am deeply honored you have chosen to spend some of your valuable time with *Customer CEO*. I trust that some of the stories I will tell you, and the ideas in them, will help you know your customers better. If you do, I guarantee you will profit by building a deeper relationship with them.

By purchasing this book, you are also partnering with me to help provide the equivalent of a lifetime of fresh drinking water to a family in desperate need of safe water in the developing world. Did you realize that more than 1.1 billion people (around one in eight of the world's population) are without access to safe water? Every day, women and children face the hardship of collecting water from long distances for their families. This filthy, contaminated water endangers lives and prevents children from growing up into strong, healthy adults. For every 500 copies of *Customer CEO* sold, I will provide a family with a Compassion's Water of Life clean water system. That's over 1 million gallons for a child and his or her family. Read more about this lifesaving mission at our website customerceoconsulting.com/water.

Here's to your great success in the coming years. May you have as much fun reading *Customer CEO* as I did writing it. And thank you for also making a real difference with Water of Life. Thanks.

Chuck Wall
February 2013

Consumers are statistics. Customers are people.
—STANLEY MARCUS

CONTENTS

Contents

PROLOGUE

An open letter to company executives everywhere:

I have been your customer for a long time, and I want you to listen to me.

You've taken me for granted as you've happily taken my money. You don't care to understand what I need to make my hectic life just a little bit better. Your products are a shadow of what they used to be, with shoddy workmanship. Your customer service is outsourced or nonexistent. You expect me to be loyal to you but you will cancel my account in a flash and later explain it was all in the fine print.

In the unlikely event you ask my opinion, you always ignore it. You continue to interrupt me with your inane ads and ridiculous offers. The only choices you really offer me anymore are lame, bad, and worse. Your values, which I once respected, have become suspect and focused on the wrong things. I've seen how you mistreat your employees, too. It seems like you now put profits over people. I don't really trust you anymore because I have become just another number you think you can spin and manipulate with your corporate speak. I am a pretty piece of data on your journey to oblivion. You don't know me, respect me, or need me.

I have given you chance after chance to listen to me and fix these things. But you don't really care. Thankfully, I have plenty of other choices of where to spend my hard-earned money. In case you hadn't noticed, there are upstart companies stepping forward to take your place every day.

And now I have a really big soapbox called the Internet. In just a few seconds thousands of like-minded people will hear me say so long, farewell, and hasta la vista, baby. I am your Customer CEO and I don't need you anymore.

Sincerely,
The Customer CEO

1

Stop, Look, and Listen

Key Customer CEO Question:

Can You Hear Me Now?

What would you do if you had lost eight hundred thousand customers and $11 billion of your investors' money in a period of a few short weeks? Hold a press conference to issue a heartfelt apology? Relocate to an undisclosed location? Resign in disgrace?

None of those were viable options for Reed Hastings, founder and CEO of Netflix. Upon suffering one of the worst business debacles in recent history, he chose to provide a nonresponse via an unfunny joke he posted on his Facebook page: "In Wyoming with 10 investors at a ranch/retreat. I think I might need a food taster. I can hardly blame them."[1]

Rather than soothing the nerves of outraged stockholders, employees, and customers, Hastings enraged them even more. After raising prices a whopping 60 percent and trying to split his company into two pieces with no advance notice, Netflix saw its stock price plummet over 75 percent. Later, in the understatement of the business year, Hastings told ABC News, "We moved too quickly. We didn't give it enough thought. We didn't give it enough explanation, enough integration, and you know, that's legitimately caused our customers to be angry."[2]

Somewhere along the way, Hastings' arrogance went into overdrive. He quit listening to his paying customers and stopped trying to understand what they wanted or needed. Not content with just two disastrous decisions, he compounded matters by failing to communicate with customers in a timely way. He never explained why he thought raising fees so much at one time was a good idea. His late apology seemed insincere and disingenuous. He didn't give his customers anything other than cheap talk. And he didn't bother to provide a way to communicate with the company. In the eyes of those affected by Hastings' poor decisions, the CEO was missing in action.

I Should Have Listened

Back in the 1970s there was an ad campaign for Southwestern Bell Telephone, one of the so-called "Baby Bells" that proliferated in the days before deregulation. Southwestern Bell emblazoned its service trucks and billboards with the letters WMBTOPCINT-BWTNTALI, which stood for "We May Be The Only Phone Company In Town But We Try Not To Act Like It." The campaign was a disaster because it was idiotic for a monopoly to pretend that it provided a great customer experience. It acted like the only phone company in town because it was. Today, companies like Netflix revel in their ability to foretell what their customers want and need based on what is now called "big data."

A modern version of the old Bell campaign might be expressed as WKEAYTYRDWUTK, for "We Know Everything About You That You Really Don't Want Us To Know." Tens of billions of dollars have been spent by companies tracking, collating, summarizing, dashboarding, and predicting customer activity. But the problem is that the information is the size of a tsunami, too vast for companies to analyze and use efficiently. This wave of information is killing both IT and marketing departments that have to try to keep up. But, in the end, big data merely reflects the "what," not the "why" of the customer experience. In other words, there has never been a time in human history when people knew so much about other people that was incomplete. It's like having a jigsaw puzzle with many missing pieces. I believe understanding why people do the things they do is the most important part of the customer experience equation.

Fortunately, I haven't been in Reed Hastings' shoes. I've had the good fortune to help great people solve some big business problems along the way. To be fair, I have made my share of mistakes as well. Some of them have been small detours; others have been bigger bumps in the road. But I can say that my biggest mistake was wasting too many years listening only to my own ideas. I liked the sound of my own voice way too much.

I should have been listening to my customers instead.

Admittedly, my radical view of hyper-listening is considered heresy in many business circles. There are business leaders, academics, and consultants who regularly warn their audiences of the folly of wasting time gathering insight from customers. "What do they know?" is the unwritten theme of many business and innovation conferences and white papers, as the experts sniff at the inability of the masses to have any clue whatsoever. The gurus sternly admonish their audiences and readers that customers don't know what they want, and wouldn't know if it hit them in the gluteus maximus. Their message is to quit wasting valuable time and money asking customers for their opinions. They believe customers are incapable of sharing anything meaningful enough to result in product innovations. They remind us that customers don't know what they don't know. To many in this prevailing business culture, customers only exist to keep consuming stuff and sending along their money; they are not to be consulted about why a company might actually keep deserving it.

Faster Horses and Fickle Customers

Two business icons are often used to support the theory that customers don't truly understand what they need. If this "Ignore the customer" philosophy was good enough for Henry Ford and Steve Jobs, shouldn't it be good enough for you? Experts often attribute this statement to Ford: "If I had asked my customers what they wanted, they would have said a faster horse."[3] They also point to various rehashed versions of statements by Jobs. Here's a quote from a 1989 interview Jobs did with *Inc.* magazine, in which he explained, "You can't just ask customers what they want and then try to give that to them. By the time you get it built, they'll want something new."[4]

Who am I to question the genius of Henry Ford and Steve Jobs? In my opinion, both were visionaries who saw things the average person could not. But there are two problems with these quotes, other than the fact that they oversimplify a complex subject. While the faster horses line is very clever, there is actually no record that Ford ever said such a thing. In his blog, Quote Investigator, researcher Garson O'Toole casts doubt on Ford as originator of the remark.[5] But the Ford "quote" makes a great presentation slide; everyone can nod his head in agreement.

In Jobs' case, it is true that he made various versions of this statement about customers' wants over a long and prosperous career. But the irony is that, because of the vision of Jobs and other technologists, nearly everything in the business world has changed since 1989. At that time, the flow of information went only one way. Technology companies' creations have empowered a new world of customers who rule companies with an iron fist. As Reed Hastings learned, today's customers can wreak havoc by destroying your carefully constructed business model in only a few hours, days, or weeks. Customers are no longer pigs at the trough, waiting to be slaughtered.

It is a myth, however, that Jobs was a one-man band. In addition to the hundreds of Apple designers who contributed to the company's success, Apple Store staff monitor the daily, almost real-time barometer of customer opinion. Also, public filings in Apple's 2012 Samsung patent lawsuit revealed that the company actually did customer research. Apparently, the research was a decisive factor in key strategic business decisions. Phil Schiller, Apple's senior vice president of global marketing, testified that Apple, in fact, conducted customer surveys of iPhone buyers that were considered "important trade secrets."[6] So the truth is, even Apple has an active and ongoing customer intelligence pipeline.

The Customer Isn't Always Right

Don't get me wrong. I don't subscribe to the old adage that customers are always right. They are often wrong. Sometimes they are mind-numbingly wrong. In 1916, the *Edison Monthly* cited people's reluctance to purchase newly designed electric fans to cool their homes when its editors wrote, "Old and tried ways of being uncomfortable proved more acceptable than new and strange comforts."[7] It is true that customers are often confused about what they believe about brands they either use or reject. That's the funny thing about perceptions; they aren't always correct. But, it's not the customer's job to be accurate in his assessments. As businesspeople, it's our job to gain customers' constant insight, feedback, and criticism in order to create better products, services, and experiences for them.

It's important to remember where we have come from. There have been three distinct marketing eras. (By marketing, I mean the activities necessary to acquire and retain customers.) First there was the production era, during which we witnessed that a good product would sell itself. With greater competition we moved into a sales era, driven by creative advertising designed to overcome customer resistance and to convince people to buy the next big thing. Today, we are rapidly entering the social era, when customers rely more upon the recommendations of their friends than on messages from the brands themselves.

As businesses, we must seek ways to more clearly understand our existing and potential customers. Some business strategists combine the end-to-end relationship between a brand and a customer into a process often called "CX" (shorthand for customer experience). Ultimately, it's how a company delivers on the total experience that drives customer loyalty and trust. In their book *Rules to Break and Laws to Follow*, Don Peppers and Martha Rogers, PhD, lay out some of the key questions every business has to answer about its customer's experience:

> What's it really like to be your customer? What is the day-in, day-out 'customer experience' your company is delivering? How does it feel to wait on hold on the phone? To open a package and not be certain how to follow the poorly translated instructions? To stand in line, be charged a fee, wait for a service call that was promised two hours ago, come back to an online shopping cart that's no longer there an hour later? Or what's it like to be remembered? To receive helpful suggestions? To get everything exactly as it was promised? To be confident that the answers you get are the best ones for you?[8]

In a nutshell, you need to think about the customer experience as no different from any successful relationship in terms of how it makes the other person feel, from beginning to end.

There are many quantitative and qualitative methodologies available for obtaining valuable insights from customers, an area often called voice-of-the-customer (VOC) research. I am proposing that you take a systematic approach to listening to and observing how your customers live their lives. Paying attention to the way they live will give you great insight into how they use your products. By stepping outside the office and into the field, you will either gain a completely different viewpoint or confirm your long-held beliefs. It is also important to invest time in learning about those who aren't your customers, because they represent potential new market opportunities. Ultimately, customer insight is where you must start in order to profit from the power of your customer.

Not Soothsayers

When discussing the idea of understanding customers, I ask my clients to remember a simple saying from childhood: Stop, look, and listen. First, stop seeing things through your own eyes. Second, begin to look at things through your customers' (and non-customers') eyes. Third, listen to them proactively. The only truly effective way to solve your business problems is to start by discovering the truth. Then you can change your behavior and move ahead. What you learn will likely amaze you, because the truth is that customers are now in control. Really in control. It is self-delusion to believe we are soothsayers who can somehow divine what customers need. Maybe Ford and Jobs were clairvoyant. But what about those of us who aren't geniuses? I am talking about business for the rest of us.

If you want more profitable growth and a consistent pathway toward innovation so you can stay ahead of the competition tomorrow, you must gain a deeper understanding of your current and future customers today. Customers are in control because of an unstoppable force: the free flow of information. Technology means companies can no longer control what people know about anything. There are no secrets. If you think there are, check out WikiLeaks. The government cannot even protect its most valued secrets. At the same time, there are more global producers of goods everywhere we look. Upstarts seem to be opening for business every day. This reality means commoditization, price wars, and shrinking value for stakeholders. Isn't the better way forward to understand customers?

By this point, you might be wondering why I am qualified to

tell you how to think about your customers. First, I'm a businessperson with thirty-plus years on the front lines, where I worked to create and retain customers every day, primarily as a serial entrepreneur and marketer. I have started companies in the manufacturing, media, advertising, technology, insurance, and consulting industries. Second, I have helped my clients sell billions of dollars of their products and services. And third, in my consulting practice, I have interviewed, observed, and surveyed more than a hundred thousand customers for my clients in virtually every type of industry. That Johnny Cash song "I've Been Everywhere" describes my travels over the past years to ask questions and deeply listen. I've talked to all kinds of people. Professional wrestling fans who believe it's real. Elvis impersonators. Italian symphony lovers. Skinny tuba players. Food truck buffs. Metaphysical vegans. Future farmers. Striking airline pilots. Overworked police detectives. Reformed criminals. Engaged, disengaged, and reengaged CEOs. In every case, some company wanted me to climb inside the heads of these customers to figure out ways to sell them something or serve them better.

Return on Insight

Customer CEO is not an economics, business strategy, market research, history, branding, or marketing book per se. While I touch on all of those important subjects, I have written the book to challenge you to think differently about your customers, your employees, and your business. This book is really a storybook intended to help guide you through the murky waters of business growth with ideas, practices, and examples that have given successful companies a decisive competitive advantage.

In this book are stories of almost three dozen companies that look to their customers as their CEOs—they are what I call Customer CEO companies. These companies understand the new power of their customers. They are winning because of their ongoing, real-time customer knowledge and engagement.

As much as I love innovation and technology, I believe customer insight is the primary driver toward a profitable, sustainable company. It is also extremely cost effective. I think you will find that your most efficient ROI is what I call *Return on Insight*. Of course, the irony is that your best insight really comes from outsight; the simple act of getting outside of yourself long enough to see and hear how your customers behave and what they believe.

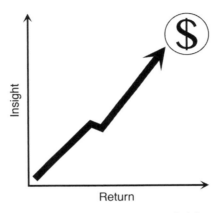

Figure 1–1: Return on Insight

Figure 1–1: Return on InsightIf customers were food, they would be onions. After we peel back a few layers, it's amazing what we discover. The deeper we go, the better the chance we'll cry, especially when we recognize the gulf that often exists between our perceptions of our customers and theirs of us.

I believe that if you understand customers better, you will profit in top-line growth, bottom-line results, and organizational excellence. All too often we have a static picture of our customers based on information made obsolete long ago. Today we must embrace a fresh and dynamic vision of our customers, a vision that shows us how they are changing and what we should do about it.

It doesn't matter if your business model is designed to serve consumers, businesses, or government agencies. If you have customers, this book is for you. *Customer CEO* will introduce you to a new way of discovering how to connect more deeply with your customers. I will introduce you to a new business strategy I call *The Customer Thinking Solution*. These ideas and strategies apply to you if you run, own, or are thinking about starting a company. If you are in sales, they will help you sell more goods or services to more customers. If you engage in that magical world called marketing, there's plenty for you on every page. I will share lessons from the field with actual quotes and observations by customers we have interviewed from coast to coast.

What's in Your Water?

The late writer David Foster Wallace told a story about two fish meandering down a little river when they came across an older fish headed the other way: "'Morning, boys. How's the water?' And the two young fish swim on for a bit, and then eventually one of them looks over at the other and says, 'What the hell is water?'"[9] The point of the fish story, of course, is that the most obvious things are often the hardest for us to see.

Customer CEO is a book about change. But it is hard to see your "water" when you are so busy struggling in the world of "what is." You have to find ways to lift yourself to a "what if" mindset. Whether you make your living in big business or small, our times are both confusing and challenging because the rules have changed. Despite the barriers we face in business today, and there are many, we must always keep moving forward. I assure you that your competitors want the upper hand. They want to defeat you and shut you down. You are playing a hardball game. You must put the power of the customer to work for you before your competitors harness that power for themselves. Your customers want and demand better customer experiences and interactions from you. If you actively engage them and provide what they need, your customers will help you achieve your dreams. This is your wake-up call. It's time to meet the Customer CEO.

2

I Am Your Customer CEO

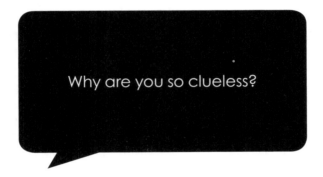

Why are you so clueless?

An old, grizzled, chain-smoking owner of nearly four hundred retail stores once grumbled to me that any idiot could succeed in business if he just understood how to "stack 'em deep and sell 'em cheap."

Another business titan who had four homes and at least as many ex-wives explained to me that customers were like mice. "If you leave a trail of crumbs," he intoned, "they'll always follow and then you just snap the trap. They're yours for the taking."

A seventy-seven-year-old founder and CEO of an automobile empire excitedly told me his "trick to success" was to use sleight of hand, like a magician might. "If you distract them with your right hand, they never see you closing them with your left. It's pure magic."

Cheap. Crumbs. Tricks. In these guys' version of business, the company controlled the customer. Ah, those were the days.

Only One Boss

Perhaps in earlier decades "stack 'em deep and sell 'em cheap" was the best way to do it. Maybe most customers *were* like mice and fell for sleight-of-hand tricks. No doubt, some still do. Imagine a pre-Google, pre-Facebook era in which customers were left in the dark, with little ability to educate themselves about companies, their policies, their product quality and prices, and what other customers thought about their user experiences.

Along the way, though, I also met more enlightened businesspeople, like retail giant Stanley Marcus, a builder of powerhouse luxury retailer Neiman Marcus, who understood this idea of profiting by pleasing people. He had learned that the right way to earn customers was to understand them better than his competitors. There was Sam Walton, the famously informal, pickup-driving founder and CEO of Walmart, who captured the idea of customer importance best when he said, "There is only one boss. The customer. And he can fire everybody in the company from the chairman on down, simply by spending his money somewhere else."[1]

Walton had vision from the beginning. He seemed to understand even then that we would be living in an era in which companies can dictate very little to a customer. There are no real secrets anymore. There are no tricks, traps, or tunes to seduce you. The information genie has escaped from the bottle and cannot be put back in. The new reality is that the customer controls the company because she can no longer be kept in the dark, being fed bite-sized spin about products and services.

Four Spinning Plates

I want to set the stage for you by taking a short trip to the Third Street Promenade in Santa Monica, California. It's just several blocks of a city street closed to vehicles, brimming with life. There are always crowds headed in and out of the shops, outdoor cafes, and wine bars. And there are street performers everywhere. A few years ago, I encountered a young Chinese acrobat who was beginning her act. I stood at the edge of the crowd watching as she produced a thin, two-foot-long wooden stick. In her left hand she balanced a plate on top of the stick and began to spin it. Balanced on a high stool, she placed another on her right foot and then a third on her left. Finally, she began to spin a fourth plate on a stick she held in her left hand. She smiled broadly as she managed those four spinning plates in perfect unison. It takes a lot of skill to balance and spin four plates at once.

The thing is, as a business executive you are spinning four plates right now, too. Your four plates represent the four dynamics driving our business world today. They can be labeled "new economy," "new competition," "new technology," and "new customer." These plates are spinning wildly out of control, and you can really only intervene with one of them: the new customer.

Figure 2–1: The Four Spinning Plates

Welcome to the age of the Customer CEO. Whether you like it or not, the Customer CEO has the power to hire you or fire you in the blink of an eye. Some businesspeople have described these new, empowered customers as barbarians at the gate. It's a challenge to prevent this siege mentality from taking root in your organization because, in many ways, the Customer CEO is not much different from a corporate CEO. Both constantly seek ways to improve their profit margins. But profit represents more than just financial success. This book will explore the ways, in addition to dollars and cents, that every business can profit by understanding its customers and the power they hold. But before looking at the relationship between profit and power, let's review how we came to this new reality.

The Power of Information

In 1907, another retail pioneer, Marshall Field, apparently said that the customer is always right. That idea has stuck for more than a century and has become an empty mantra echoed from the boardroom to the business school classroom. Everyone loves to say it, but how many really believe it? The truth is that customers once had little power to control much of anything. They could decide to do a transaction with a particular company or not, but they often had few choices. Companies controlled the flow of information regarding products, services, and pricing. They set the agenda for the experience they wanted the customer to have. It was a top-down world. Like the three real businesspeople I described at the opening of this chapter, most companies viewed their customers with complete disregard because they could.

Look at the baby boomer generation and how things have changed over their lifetimes. These were the post-World War II babies, born between 1946 and 1964. From the 1960s through the 1980s big media controlled the news people received, the programs they watched, and the music they heard. It was a three-network world, where CBS, NBC, and ABC dominated the relatively new medium of television. Most cities had both morning and evening newspapers with high circulations. There were a handful of dominant radio stations in each market, and the stations were often owned by the newspaper. If an upstart brand wanted to advertise to a nation of excited consumers, it was at a competitive disadvantage because it couldn't afford the high cost of national advertising. Many innovative brands were relegated to smaller regions of the country, as bigger companies effectively kept them in check.

By the early 1990s, media deregulation began to break the stranglehold on the flow of information held by a handful of media empires. Many newspapers began to lose their popularity, as busy boomers had less time to spend reading them. By the middle part of the decade, an information revolution was brewing. The Internet began to bubble up slowly. On the web, America Online was the first brand to break through. In my own customer research regarding the Internet, as late as 1997, 85 percent of those surveyed thought AOL *was* the Internet. They were afraid to venture too far away from AOL's home page. No way were these pioneers going to venture into cyberspace by typing in some strange domain name in something called a "browser window."

Meanwhile, dozens of new cable television networks were getting their programs and commercials into the homes of eighty million cable-ready households for a fraction of the cost associated with major networks. The stranglehold of the few was starting to loosen. By the 2000s the information stream was shifting in entirely new, unexpected, and creative directions. New digital media, search engines, online video, text messaging, mobile devices, and social media were shaping the information landscape in ways unknown to human history. A new warning echoed around boardroom tables all across the world: this free-flowing planet of information would be the Achilles' heel of any business that ignored it.

As technology has pushed us further and further from the days of crumbs and tricks, business has also been roiled by unprecedented economic headwinds that have affected virtually every type of customer. Businesses serving the middle market have suffered, while bargain basement operators and high-end merchants have often done much better. The new world economy continues to be marked by significant headwinds, including prolonged high unemployment, inflation, record national and personal debt, and a decline in personal income.

Here's the thing: the macro economy is as emotional as it is structural. Customers who feel positive about the future are much more likely to spend money or go into debt for a larger purchase. If they don't, you already know what happens. It's not pretty. These economic and psychological factors are why it has never been more important to have a crystal-clear understanding of the customer.

Where Are You Going?

You would not begin a journey without some kind of road map for how to get where you wanted to go. Yet, many companies are still using very old assumptions. Your current and potential customers have changed dramatically over the past fifty years. And because of technology, they are now changing faster than ever before. Here's one example.

When my consulting firm was engaged by a retail client a few years ago, the president was interested in understanding what noncustomers really knew about his brand and why they were shopping elsewhere. He was convinced that the reason was related to price because of an informal survey the company had done a decade earlier. That survey had revealed that price was the most important consideration for customers in choosing a store brand. It became his raison d'être. These results were set in concrete, and he couldn't hear anything else. He had built his entire brand strategy on the low-price premise. But, overall, sales results were flat or down, and a new VP of marketing convinced the company president to actually talk to some noncustomers.

Our research told us that noncustomers for this brand didn't even think about this store or the prices because they didn't *trust him*, the company's president. They didn't trust him because he insisted on appearing in his own television commercials. Although he was on camera for less than five seconds, that was all the time it took for him to undermine his brand. Why? His on-camera role consisted of appearing in a blatantly expensive suit displaying a less-than-sincere smile. He was neither believable nor likeable. That made him appear untrustworthy, so customers took their money somewhere else.

New Customers May Not Be Who You Think

If old habits die hard, so does old information. Executives get something in their heads and claim to really know their customers, but often the facts don't back them up. Many business leaders range in age from mid-forties to early sixties. This means that they grew up in a different America. Their built-in perceptions were learned long ago. These long-held beliefs are why so many businesspeople are resistant to change. Why fix what's not broken? But, there's often a lot broken. It starts with a poor understanding of customers as they are today. Here are a few examples.

Since 1960, customers are 27 percent older. They are four times more educated. The number of customers who are married has dropped by 30 percent. The average person today weighs 17 percent more than the average person did in 1960. Customers are seven times more likely not to have any formal religious affiliation.[2] Nearly half do not pay any federal income tax.[3] The majority of homeowners have reset their expectations of home ownership because they do not expect the value of their homes to increase for at least three years.[4] Nearly 70 percent of Americans use search engines.[5] The percentage of consumers who use both social media and search engines in their buying process has risen to 48 percent.[6] Consumer confidence is lower than ever. Customers don't trust institutions, including big business and government. Yet, my own research has proven that Americans remain, by and large, aspirational and optimistic; generally, they want to be left alone to pursue happiness the way they wish.

If you are looking for a straight-line solution to understanding today's customer, forget about it. It doesn't exist. Knowing the Customer CEO is like being on a roller coaster. One minute you can see what's just ahead but then, without warning, the bottom can drop out. Customers are competitive, calculating, complicated, and confusing. They can be crazy and caustic, immature, inexperienced, and unqualified. Their absolute sense of entitlement may upset you. Customer CEOs aren't always right. Their perceptions may be skewed by a lens of their own making. They don't always tell the truth. Some Customer CEOs have gone too far and become customer vigilantes. They will use your brick-and-mortar store as a showroom; they'll find a better price online and not give you a second thought. Who cares if you are losing money? Not their problem.

We are at tipping point. We have moved to a world of fully empowered, in-your-face customers who use technology on their personal devices to decide instantly where to award their dollars and their loyalty. Think of social media turning into social commerce. We can imagine a day in the very near future when a business traveler can comparison shop hotels, make reservations, and even file expense reports in real time through a single, fully integrated mobile app.

This is a confounding time of transition. In recent studies of business, we see consistent concern expressed by CEOs who no longer understand their customers.[7] They aren't sure how to match their innovation efforts with real-world unmet customer needs.[8] They reluctantly admit that the customer is in charge but they don't know how to change.[9] The default position for many is to do nothing and hope that business changes back or somehow becomes easier. Sadly, hope is not a successful strategy.

Businesses of every type face significant hurdles when it comes to understanding their customers and how to serve them.

Many people are absorbed by a celebrity culture in which people are known for who they are, not what they have actually done. College administrators complain that Gen Y students are incapable of making decisions, often because of omnipresent "helicopter parents" who attempt to micro-manage their children.[10] These same parents have raised their offspring to expect equal outcomes, arranging contests so that everyone wins a ribbon regardless of the effort put forth. Adolescent men are delaying growing up for as long as possible, preferring to live at home and play video games well into their twenties. Pollster John Zogby has referred to them as "CENGAs" for "college-educated, not going anywhere."[11]

Many millennials are obsessed with texting and tweeting, often at the expense of actual conversations.[12] Human resource executives report overt antisocial behavior during interviews, including some candidates taking phone calls and texting. Many people are worried about the kind of country their children will grow up in. How will mountains of debt and the prospect of higher taxes ahead change customers in relationship to the businesses they want to connect with?

On the other hand, technology has allowed people of every age to innovate, design, and create solutions. Look at the success of the Apple App Store. There are more than seven hundred thousand individual apps, and the number is growing daily.[13] An entirely new breed of "entrepreneurs on the cheap" is emerging. These societal trends are critical to your business success and your own career. How can you navigate these choppy waters and turn many of these people into loyal ambassadors for your brand? If you can figure it out, they have the power to help you reach cult status almost overnight. I know these things because I have observed and listened to customers almost every day for more than three decades. I study what people think and how they communicate. I can tell you, firsthand, that businesses have widespread misconceptions about customers, about what they believe in, and about what they are looking for from companies.

You may choose to mock, scorn, or trick them, but this book's core message is that you'd better not ignore them any longer. They are shouting. They also have cash, credit cards, and computers. Are you listening?

Breaking Free

From a business point of view, how can you help your customers live the lives they want and profit in the process? Author and father of disruptive innovation Clayton Christensen explains it this way in his book *Seeing What's Next*: "We live our lives in circumstances. During the course of the day, problems arise and we look around to hire products to solve these problems."[14] Getting the job done. This seems logical and is common sense. When we think about business this way, it changes everything. It's no longer just a product or service for sale; it's the customer's higher purpose.

Customers lead busy lives full of barriers and challenges. They need to solve these problems, so they hire products and services along the way to accomplish just that. Some jobs are purely functional, like getting a flat tire repaired on your car. Other jobs are emotional, like the way the car you drive makes you feel or the message it conveys to others. There are also ancillary jobs, like deciding what kind of aftermarket GPS device to use. This requires deeper insight into our customers. But many organizations fight the notion that they should pay attention to this way of thinking because they have products and services to sell in the marketplace. I believe there are three primary reasons that organizations fail to pay attention to their customers.

Build It and They Will Come

In the movie *Field of Dreams*, Kevin Costner's character heard voices that convinced him to build a ballpark in the middle of an Iowa cornfield. Hollywood loves to tell a great story, but in real life that would be either crazy or egomaniacal. We tend to think we are right because of our gut feelings or past experience. We believe we have experience that mystically supersedes the market reality. Remember my old retail client in the thousand-dollar suit?

Other times, we believe we are a combination of clairvoyant and mad scientist, creating something that no one else has ever thought of. It may work once in a while, when a genius like Steve Jobs comes along. But what about the rest of us mere mortals? Ego run amok is killing business, as we saw with Reed Hastings and the Netflix fiasco.

B-School Bots

The second reason companies fight the idea of customer insight is an unhealthy reliance on what we business executives have been taught by our professors, mentors, and the experts. Christensen loves to ask his audiences to raise their hands if they've gone to business school. He congratulates them for this incredible achievement and proceeds to explain that everything they learned was wrong. He explains that the silo mentality that most businesses have is restraining growth and innovation. The better world of business must be based on making it easier for customers to accomplish what they were already trying to get done. When you leave the customer out of the equation, you greatly decrease your odds of success.

The Trophy Case

Remember those trophy cases at your high school filled with dusty medals, trophies, and awards for great academic or athletic achievements from days long gone? Maybe your son or daughter—or even you—has a box of ribbons stuffed away on the top shelf of a closet. Those awards are a snapshot of an achievement earned a long time ago. Not to diminish those memories, but the trophy case is a metaphor for being stuck in the past. You know, longing for the good old days when life was simple and customers behaved themselves. Trophy case thinking is simply denial of a new reality.

A New Order of Things

You have to break away from ego, from what you've been taught, and from denial of reality. These three are like Kryptonite slowly sapping your strength and eventually killing your business. Every businessperson knows deep down that there is hidden value and deep insight to be gained by observing and listening to customers instead of herself.

In this book we will discuss customers, meaning those people or organizations that you currently do business with. The goal is for you to retain as many of the profitable ones as possible, because the cost of replacing them continues to grow. We will also refer to future customers. These are noncustomers you would like to serve. I believe that most of us have yet to meet our best customers. *Customer CEO* will help you find them.

Niccolò Machiavelli, the famous Italian writer and philosopher, wisely wrote, "There is nothing more difficult to take in hand, more perilous to conduct, or more uncertain in its success, than to take the lead in the introduction of a new order of things."[15] You have to choose the kind of company you will be in the Customer CEO age. It requires a purposeful shift from a nontraditional approach.

The Noncustomer CEO company says:

- Here's what we can sell them.
- Here's what we will tell them.
- Here's what we *have to* do to create relationships with them.
- Here's what we're willing to spend to "acquire" them.
- This is how we will separate them from more of their money.

On the other hand, a Customer CEO company asks:

- What are the questions we need to ask to understand both our current and future customers?

- What can we do to help them solve their problems?
- What are the ways we can complement their lives instead of complicating them?
- What are the boundaries they want to set for our relationship?
- What is the customer willing to invest in our products, services, and experiences?

A Simple Formula for Moving Forward

This book is based on a simple, three-step formula for you.

Customer Power + Active Engagement = Transformative Profit

Simply put, when you clearly understand your customers' core needs (which I call their powers) and actively engage them where they are with specific strategies, you will profit in multiple ways and thrive for years to come. *Customer CEO* lays out the nine powers that customers possess. I will show you the ways your organization can profit from these powers if you have the right strategies in place to actively engage these customers.

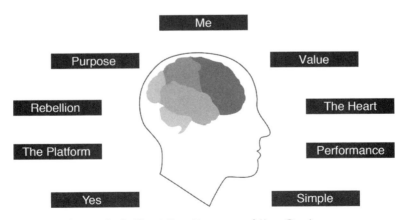

Figure 2–2: The Nine Powers of the Customer

It should be clear by now that there has been a tectonic shift in power between companies and customers. The customer is the new power at the epicenter of the enterprise. *Customer CEO* will tell you that sometimes you have to go back to leap ahead. In a customer-driven company, the organization is more decentralized and management is flatter. The people on the front line have more responsibility.

You can only be as big as the problems you can solve for customers. Businesses that refuse to understand that the customer is in charge are willfully blind and sadly deserve their inevitable demise. Imagine what the economy could be if every company tapped into the unrealized value of engaging its customers. It's time to turn the business world, and your company, upside down by engaging the power of the Customer CEO.

3

The Power of Me

What's in it for me?

On the July 4th holiday in 1989 Americans celebrated 223 years of independence. Big cities and small towns across the fruited plains celebrated with the usual array of parades, cookouts, and fireworks. On that holiday Tuesday, no one was aware that history would soon move its colossal hand. In just four months, the wall that had separated nearly three generations of German families would fall. The shock waves generated by this single great event would unleash the energy to reunify Germany and realign Eastern Europe, and would lead to the eventual disintegration of the Soviet Union. Geopolitical power would shift forever. Markets would be created, dictators would fall, and the wonder of freedom would spring eternal. Big things happened in 1989.

Something else important happened that July 4th holiday in America, though it went unnoticed by most people. Another history-making event occurred that would reshape American culture. It would give voice to a new group of people not usually given a significant platform. That event was the debut episode of a little-noticed television program that would eventually impact tens of millions of people for most of the next decade.

It was July 5, 1989, that America first laid eyes on *The Seinfeld Chronicles*. If you missed that first episode, you might have come to know it by its shortened name, *Seinfeld*. And, like the fall of the Berlin Wall, the show would see, over nine years and 180 episodes, more markets created, more dictators defeated, and even more freedom brought forth.

Apparently, I was one of the few eyewitnesses to that first episode. Viewership was so low that NBC almost passed on the series.[1] But after watching the *Seinfeld* pilot episode, I was hooked. That's because, for me, it was like watching a focus group. The program had captured the essence of what I was already seeing in many of the people I interviewed. However, the TV-viewing audience, such as it was, didn't seem to find much worth watching. Early research described the pilot episode as weak, noting, "None of the supports were particularly liked...George was negatively viewed as a 'wimp' who was only mildly amusing—viewers said he whined and did not like his relationship with Jerry."[2]

Jerry, Elaine, Kramer, George, Newman, and the other various neurotic characters we met brought self-centeredness to a new art form. In a slight twist to the old joke, if you looked up the definition of the word "selfish" in the dictionary, you would see a picture of the *Seinfeld* cast. And it is in these characters that we meet the first power of the Customer CEO: The Power of Me.

Seinfeld was revolutionary in television entertainment because there were no happy endings each week. The producers stuck to a fast rule of "no hugging, no learning." From the beginning of the sitcom genre in the late 1940s, with shows like *I Love Lucy*, a happy ending was mandatory. Every character conflict was neatly wrapped up in a bow by the end of the half-hour episode. But Jerry Seinfeld and his cocreator, Larry David, decided to go a different way. They portrayed people more like they were in reality. And the audience loved it because every week they got a small glimpse of themselves.

Seinfeld brilliantly captured the essence of the Power of Me. It's all about moi. What matters most is what I think. My opinion matters more than yours. My self-interest is at the root of my daily decisions in virtually every area of life. I'm in charge. I worship myself and I expect you to do it, too. If you want my business you will listen to me.

Figure 3–1: Customer Understanding

Often, the Power of Me is rooted in the simple fact that these customers have the need to exert control over some aspect of their lives. Who better to boss around than the companies they give their money to? This sense of control can quickly grow out of control and become dictatorial. No doubt, an entitlement mentality drives some of this phenomenon. But here's the thing: these self-obsessed people also have the ability to broadcast their opinions about the companies with which they deal. The Customer CEO owns devices loaded with social media tools that give her the ability to amplify her individual voice into a movement overnight. Customers can and will do it when you least expect it. Social media uprisings are now common when organizations lose their way.

Crazy Customers

How should a company think about this Power of Me? Unfortunately, far too often I see an attitude of "Our customers are crazy." Recently, a chief marketing officer of a large insurance company told me that their "consumers" were "certifiably insane." He based his conclusions upon a recent customer satisfaction survey in which his company had performed quite poorly. He meant it. "They don't even understand how their policies work," he sniffed.

Because his company distributes its products through independent agents, he sees the agents as his real customers. Those pesky drivers, horrible homeowners, and lousy life insurance policyholders just consume. They pay their little premiums and file their petty claims. Sadly, his attitude is not that unusual. It reflects the attitude often held in the C-suite in enterprises of every size. Rather than taking the opportunity to teach customers about their policies, it was just easier to dismiss them. Of course, the insurance company has no problem cashing those premium checks every month.

I believe the word "consumer" demeans the people who choose to do business with your brand or anyone representing your brand, like an agent. In its original meaning, a consumer was someone who squandered or wasted, hardly a respectful way to describe a person on whom your business depends. Customer is the more honorable word, acknowledging that the person had a choice of companies to deal with. In today's world, choice is an understatement. If you think of your customers the way the insurance CMO does, you are making a big mistake. Simply put, customers are the people who write the check, debit the accounts, or barter the chickens. They are the me.

I understand how easy it can be to fall into the trap of blaming the customer. The increased stress most executives feel is daunting. Between unrelenting technology, increased competition, and greater pressure for positive financial performance, someone is bound to get the blame. The easiest target is George Costanza, the demanding, unreasonable customer hardly worthy of our valuable time.

I am reminded of a story my father told me many years ago. He sold industrial-grade construction products. His customers were general contractors and institutions like schools and hospitals. He said that every year during the holidays, he wrote out a list of all the available customers in his region. As the year progressed, he would cross off the names of various "scoundrels, thieves, and liars" he chose to no longer do business with due to some disagreement, real or imagined. Eventually, most of the names had been crossed off. As the holidays came around again, Dad would swallow his pride and repeat the same cycle. He would laugh and say, "Son, if you think you're ever in charge, you're kidding yourself. You'll always work for your customers, so you might as well enjoy it."

The George Quiz

Let's return to George Costanza. In one memorable episode, he needed to read *Breakfast at Tiffany's* for a book club he'd joined.[3] But in typical George fashion, he thought that actually reading the book required too much effort. He decided to watch the movie, but learned the video store's only copy had been checked out. George invited himself to the home of the people who'd rented the video and convinced them to let him watch the movie with them. As an uninvited guest, George felt he was entitled to something to "nosh," like popcorn.

George Costanza was, no doubt, everyone's customer from hell. He attempted to cheat at every opportunity. I lost count of the number of restaurants and stores George was thrown out of over the entirety of the series. Do customers like George deserve our respect or our wrath?

Let's do a quick exercise I call The George Quiz. Get two

pieces of paper. I want you to write down on the first page what you really think of your customers. No, I mean *really* think of them. Picture George and everything you despise about him. Feel free to take a few minutes to get this off your chest. Go ahead and vent. Write down every adjective and phrase that comes to mind.

Okay, now that you have done that, I want you to set that page aside and write down what you think your customers really think of you on the other page. How did you do? I bet that was a much shorter list. What's really going on? Many businesspeople have a complete lack of respect for their customers. It's absolutely true that we are living in a new age of societal narcissism. For example, if you have ever been to an NBA game, you know that it is not unusual to observe ordinary people going to extraordinary lengths to get themselves on the Kiss-Me Cam during time outs. Or consider the thousands of YouTube videos that people post celebrating themselves and their own opinions.

This is the new reality of the Power of Me. From the customer's point of view, he is always right. To ignore that is shortsighted. To continue to emphasize your superiority demonstrates arrogance. If you desire your customers' business, you need to rewire your thinking to the Power of Me. "What's in it for me?" is the essential question every customer asks herself, even unconsciously, when faced with virtually every decision.

Am I suggesting that to grow your business the only hope is to appeal to a bunch of selfish narcissists like Jerry, Elaine, George, and Kramer? No. But as businesspeople we must be completely honest with ourselves. Most people are so busy taking care of themselves, their families, and their jobs that the companies they do business with only register as tiny flickers on their radar screens. Our ads and websites that scream, "Look at us and our new widgets" usually fall on deaf ears because people are primarily focused on what's in it for them. Companies that continue to stay centered on their own profits are missing where the market is moving. How can you profit from the Power of Me? It starts by getting upside down.

Reframe the Issue

A designer friend of mine loved to pick up interesting prints and original paintings at estate sales for next to nothing. The art could usually be found in well-worn frames. She had the vision most design stars possess to see the possibilities in the picture that could be highlighted simply by reframing it. In most cases, she was able to resell the pieces for many times what she had paid.

I believe the same principle applies to business. By reframing long-held beliefs about customers, my clients have been able to see new and simpler ways to visualize the position of the Customer CEO.

I designed a simple visual tool I call the Upside-Down Org Chart. It's a two-box organizational chart that illustrates the Power of Me. The top box simply says, "The Customer." The lower box says, "Everyone required to serve them with excellence." I believe this chart paints a simple picture for the entire organization that clearly communicates that the customer is really in charge.

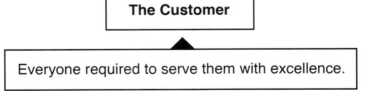

Figure 3–2: The Upside-Down Org Chart

If you do not really believe that your customers are in charge, you are being stubborn. The reality is that your existing and potential customers can choose to do business however they want. You are merely one option in lives filled with too many choices, distractions, and debts. They *can* live without you.

You might continue to succeed even if you occasionally throw a George Costanza out on his ear, but you cannot afford to do that very often. Let's return to George's complaints, irrational as they might be. Could you learn something about your products, services, and experiences by forcing yourself to proactively engage with George? What if he actually has a valid complaint? Will you hear it through the barriers you have erected to tune him out?

The Lesson of Smiling Faces

Who hires these people? They come to the table and try to sell you stuff you don't want before you've even had time to look at the menu. And I don't care if your name is Heather or how much sparkle you have on your uniform.

Miguel, El Paso, Texas
Participant in focus group about restaurants

After I worked with a client in downtown San Diego, I took a long walk. I was just a few yards from the Pacific Ocean. My little jaunt brought me to Lighthouse Ice Cream and Yogurt in Ocean Beach. I needed no excuse to try the local fare, so I ordered the fresh ice cream waffles. They were really quite remarkable but I was more interested in the posters that hung on the walls, which featured thousands of photos of their customers' smiling faces. The manager explained that they had a Lighthouse tradition of snapping photos of their customers. She said that I was looking at more than ten years' worth of happy customers. Obviously, it took much dedication to continue a tradition like this for so long. I asked her why they kept doing it. Her answer gave me great insight into how every company can make the Power of Me very tangible:

It's our daily wake-up call that without these customers we have nothing. We honor them by putting them up on our walls. After they leave we may never see them again because many are tourists, but their smiling faces are a constant reminder that we are here to serve them.

The Lighthouse lesson taught me that we could all harness the Power of Me with simple rituals. By keenly focusing on literal pictures of our customers, we cannot help but be reminded of their points of pain in life. It is our job to help solve the pain and move them to gain. Dynamic customer walls are a constant visual reminder of our Customer CEOs and that they are the reason we are in business.

Meatballs for Everyone

My husband and I bought a new sofa, loveseat, and bedroom set for our new house at [a big, locally owned store]. That's when the salesman told us it would take several days to deliver, plus there would be a $100 delivery charge. We said you got to be kidding so he said we could take it with us if we had to have it today. I asked him if he knew how to get a couch into a Toyota Corolla.

Margaret, Seattle, Washington
Participant in a focus group about furniture stores

Anyone who has ever gone to an Ikea store cannot say that it is the best experience. You usually have to drive a considerable distance to get there, find parking, and begin the slog through myriad twists and turns in the hope of capturing the particular item you want. Once you have it, the trek back to the cash register is a long and winding one through endless displays of bookcases, kitchen accessories, and ready-to-hang prints of city skylines. Plan on devoting the better part of an afternoon to finding that $15 lamp you want for your bedside table. So what does Ikea grasp about the Power of Me that makes people willing to do this?

The Ikea big business idea is: "We shall offer a wide range of well-designed, functional home furnishing products at prices so low that as many people as possible will be able to afford them."[4]

How has this vision paid off? Over one half billion annual shoppers cannot all be wrong. With U.S. sales of over $3 billion and nearly $20 billion globally, Ikea obviously grasps the Power of Me. Each store stocks more than twelve thousand different household furnishing products. In fact, Ikea serves more than 150 million Swedish meatballs each year in its stylish in-store eateries.[5]

Simply put, Ikea means good design at a low price. And people know it. In 1985, founder Ingvar Kamprad confirmed his embrace of the Power of Me: "We have decided once and for all to side with the many. What is good for our customers is also, in the long run, good for us."[6]

Company legend has it that in 1956, Ikea employee number four, Gillis Lundgren, attempted to squeeze a table into the trunk of his small Volvo. Frustrated that the protruding legs would not allow the trunk lid to close, he made a radical decision that would transform the fledgling company forever: he broke the legs off and threw them in the trunk! This accidental innovation gave birth to Ikea's major point of distinction: flat-packed furniture they call ready-to-assemble (RTA).

Flat packing put the Power of Me on display for all to see. Ikea's customers become active partners, not just people looking for low prices. Ikea's customers agree to take their furniture home where they will assemble it. Ikea honors its customers by dramatically reducing the price point. As one sign posted throughout the store states: "We're obsessed with packing things flat. Why? Because you can take them home today!"

Listening to the Listeners

When I'm in the mood for listening to a certain artist I can't ever seem to hear them enough, morning, noon, and night. But then it's like a break-up: I don't want to hear from them again for a really, really long time.

Maria, Los Angeles, California
Participant in a focus group about radio

Tim Westergren's work through the Music Genome Project, a patented algorithm that scours hundreds of musical attributes (like rhythm, tempo, texture, tonality, pitch, key, and harmonies), evolved into what is now known as Pandora, the equivalent of the most sophisticated online radio station in the world. As the website explains, "Each song in the Music Genome Project is analyzed using up to 450 distinct musical characteristics by a trained music analyst. These attributes capture not only the musical identity of a song, but also the many significant qualities that are relevant to understanding the musical preferences of listeners."[7] For more than a decade, the Music Genome team analyzed music across every genre. The extensive database means Pandora can deliver a totally unique experience to every listener, resulting in a customized Power of Me radio experience that features the songs you love.

In essence, Pandora handed the keys to listeners, who could pick the artists they wanted to hear, when they wanted to hear them. Pandora essentially created an "artificial intelligence" method of programming an online radio station. This new way to listen to music brought listeners streaming in as word spread of its unique way of predicting what you wanted to hear. Pandora embraced the Power of Me.

Westergren came from the school of listening to the listeners: he said, "It's the playlist, stupid."[8] From start-up to nearly $150 million in revenue in just three years, Pandora honored its Customer CEOs. The firm recognizes that each customer has completely unique musical tastes. Pandora understood and respected that listeners also quickly grew tired of the same artists and songs and might prefer classic rock on Tuesday but love classical performances on Wednesday. The company stayed plugged in to every listener's Power of Me because the technology allowed it.

People I have met from Pandora describe the intense feedback loop they have with listeners who aren't shy about weighing in with what they think about the service. Pandora wanted to know how listeners engaged with the site on a real-time basis. They fine-tuned their offerings through better matches with similar artists or songs with texture and tempo the listener liked. Pandora created a virtual radio station where every listener was in control. Westergren's vision was to put the control solely in the hands of the listeners, so they could become their own radio station program director: "With Pandora, we have hundreds of millions of different radio stations, and something like 90,000 artists and three quarters of a million songs."[9]

Westergren says, "It's the reason Pandora has grown so fast—because we are bringing people back to music."[10] But, Pandora's future is uncertain. Traditional radio broadcasters are rolling out new online streaming options that give listeners many more options. These local stations have large existing audiences and the support of local advertisers that need the medium to tell their stories in a cost-efficient way. These factors give traditional broadcasters a strong financial footing and an economic advantage over Pandora. They also have the advantage of being local, something Pandora cannot compete with. Whatever the outcome, the Customer CEO listener has more power today than ever before.

A Seat at the Table

I completely understand why Borders closed. Every time I went in there they had to "special order" whatever I needed. I asked them to e-mail me when it came in, but they said they would call me. They never did. The last time, they sent my book back before I could pick it up. They didn't have any respect for their customers and it showed.

Brenda, Orlando, Florida
Participant in a customer interview about bookstores

Amazon founder Jeff Bezos has a video posted on YouTube in which he says there are just three things he knows about business: "Obsess over customers, invent, and think long term."[11] No company has gone further to embrace the Power of Me than Amazon. Bezos created the idea of "the empty chair." He loves to keep one seat at executive meetings open to represent Amazon's customer, whom he calls "the most important person in the room."[12]

With nearly 175 million customers and over $48 billion in sales, Bezos has created a culture deeply invested in the Power of Me.[13] The firm has more than sixty-five thousand employees, and they are consistently reminded that they exist only to serve customers.[14] As Amazon has grown past its bookselling-only days into other major retail categories, this is more than a nice idea. It is a disciplined strategy benchmarked against several hundred metrics. With thousands of hourly customer interactions, Amazon can learn in real time what each customer wants and doesn't want. According to *Forbes*, "They hate delays, defects, and out-of-stock products."[15] Rather than reject customers as too needy or difficult, Amazon embraces them. The company seeks every miniscule opportunity to learn and improve its performance. This is why Amazon consistently has one of the top customer satisfaction scores in the world. According to the ForeSee E-Retail Satisfaction Index, "Amazon continues to set the standard for e-retailers. Amazon's score sets a record as the highest score ever attained by a retailer measured in this Index."[16]

Bezos craves customer input, especially negative feedback, believing that it's the best way to improve. This gets to the heart of the problem with most companies: it is simply too painful or difficult to hear the truth. It is much easier to simply live in denial or appoint a committee to look into the problem. Let's face a difficult truth here: our tendency as business leaders is to first sweep the dirt under the rug. Maybe no one will find out. We've got new stuff to sell today and we believe we can do it despite our customers.

The question is whether the technology that built Amazon will become a double-edged sword. Will the company inevitably succumb to the temptation to stack 'em deep and sell 'em cheap? Amazon is increasingly competing with its own two million small business partners who sell a variety of goods on the site. New software, pioneered on the trading floors of the stock market, allows nearly real-time price adjustments as these sellers continually attempt to undercut one another in a practice dubbed "robo-pricing." Many longtime Amazon partners feel that Amazon has stacked the deck in favor of the house.[17] The lesson is that companies, no matter how powerful, must continue to be vigilant in their quest to be Customer CEO-friendly. If not, it's only a matter of time before someone will begin chipping away, customer by unhappy customer.

Don't #$*!% Me Over

I flew American nearly every month for over twenty years. But, at some point they changed from valuing me as a person to treating me like a piece of meat, just to fill a seat. It got to a point where every flight was some kind of ordeal where I had to fight for just basic service. I avoided Southwest like the plague, but once I tried them, it was easy to switch. With all the stress of travel, its nice to actually see airline employees who smile, not scowl.

Dean, Dallas, Texas
Participant in a focus group about travel

Southwest Airlines sold me on their "Company Plane" idea hook, line, and sinker many years ago.[18] I have lost track of the hundreds of Southwest flights I have taken across America. But, to clearly see the Power of Me in action, it's important to see a personal example, not a business strategy.

Several years ago, Joseph Rodriguez, a young account executive for our marketing firm, excitedly called me. While deplaning at Dallas Love Field, he was greeted by Southwest's then-CEO and founder, Herb Kelleher. He was thrilled to meet this business legend, as the famous CEO engaged him in personal conversation for several minutes, asking Rodriguez about his job and what had brought him to Dallas that day. Kelleher showed a true attitude of gratitude and thanked Rodriguez for his business. Upon his return, Rodriguez sent a personal note to Kelleher. Not long after, a personal letter from Kelleher arrived, thanking him for letting Southwest have the honor of flying him. Rodriguez had the letter enlarged and framed. It hung in his office for several years. Herb Kelleher had turned the Power of Me completely to his advantage. He made a new friend and a lifelong fan because he recognized the Power of Me.

One secret of Southwest's success has been the airline's almost uncanny ability to speak to its customers in their own language through letters as well as advertising. Southwest has always believed that communication was the beginning of understanding. Rather than focusing on the usual beauty shots of planes flying through crystal-clear blue skies with golden rays of sunshine dancing off the wings, Southwest has always connected through humor. The company has never taken itself too seriously because it felt that the traveler would share and enjoy the joke.

Contrast that approach with the out-of-step messaging of the last twenty years from United, American, and Delta. They seem aloof and impersonal. The people who run Southwest have always understood that one of the secrets to building rapport with customers is how you answer the "Who would I like to have a beer with?" question. At Southwest, passengers would love to have a beer with Herb or other company leaders because they believe the Southwest team is funny and approachable. In the early days, Southwest advertised free whiskey if you would fly them. In a memorable full-page *Wall Street Journal* ad, the airline printed a large coupon stating "Don't #$*!% Me Over."[19] The ad proudly announced that Southwest was the only airline accepting this coupon. This tongue-in-cheek ad poked fun at other airlines that were nickel and diming their passengers with extra charges for luggage, snacks, pillows, and blankets, brilliantly tapping into a rich vein of customer discontent. It was like whispering, "We're in this together!"

In their book *Nuts!* authors Kevin and Jackie Freiberg explain that Southwest's marketing team was fanatical about connecting with customers through core principles, including "Take the competition seriously, but not yourself," "Make every employee a living advertisement," and "Make flying fun."[20] At Southwest, even the advertising recognizes the power of the Customer CEO.

Profiting from the Power of Me

In the summer of 1967, a song by rhythm and blues singer Aretha Franklin shot to the top of the charts. She turned "Respect" into one of the most memorable songs in music history. Aretha's R-E-S-P-E-C-T became a liberation theme for women. Your customers just want the same R-E-S-P-E-C-T. This is the key strategy to profiting from the Power of Me. And the way you will profit is by creating a bond of trust between you and your customers.

To see how important this concept is, let's return to 2004. That was the year media maven and business magnate Martha Stewart was convicted of obstructing justice and lying to investigators about the sale of some stock. I was stunned to learn how much this single event affected the attitudes of customers. In a Los Angeles focus group for an insurance company, a woman named Cerrita summed up public sentiment: "I've been watching Martha for more years than I can remember. Now, when I see her on TV, I just say you are a big fake. I can't trust you. These rich celebrities and business people just manipulate the system to enrich themselves. So why would I ever trust an insurance company when I can't even trust Martha Stewart?"

Good question. To Cerrita, Martha's conduct reflected poorly on everyone in business. The rest of the people in that series of focus groups agreed with this sentiment. This is because we have battered our customers with hundreds of reasons to actively distrust us.

The Edelman 2011 Trust Barometer Global Opinion Leader Study found that lack of trust is a barrier to change.[21] Trust is a protective agent for our enterprises. The report describes a clear transformation of trust, changing from a primary focus on profit and the desire to control information to a new "Trust Architecture." This new approach is made up of three equal elements: profit with purpose (the what), transparency (the how), and engagement (the where). This is a good test for every company to take. What purpose do your customers believe you have, other than trying to separate them from their money? Is your company believable and do you consistently demonstrate that through your public communications and deeds? And are you willing to meet customers where they are?

The easiest way to meet customers where they are is to shower them with respect. Customer CEO companies like Lighthouse Ice Cream, Ikea, Pandora, Amazon, and Southwest Airlines actively engage with their customers in a number of ways, including the following ones.

Watch Your Language

How do you refer to your customers? What do you call them? Are they pests or partners? Do you believe they are even worthy of your respect? We all learn bad habits by allowing ourselves to dwell in the short-term negative reactions we have to negative experiences. Snap out of it! Starting today, re-respect your customers. Start by talking about them inside the organization with respectful language.

Fix the Top Five Customer Problems

Customers are tired of lip service, platitudes, and empty promises. There is no bigger sign of disrespect than ignoring the clear pain points that you have learned from your customers. Think about it this way: How would you feel if you took a customer survey and identified key issues, but nothing ever came of it?

Tell Customers Who to Contact

One of the biggest problems we consistently hear about is customer runaround. It doesn't matter whether this happens on the company's premises, in a contact center, or on a website, customers don't know who they should contact or how to get in touch with that person. Unanswered voice mails and e-mails are the norm, not the exception. Would you tolerate this kind of attitude?

How about job titles that seem like they're from some other planet, designed to make the employee feel better? One CEO I know decided to change the title of anyone who faces the customer to "problem solver." That's it, nothing else. We shouldn't force our customers to figure out how to communicate with us. We must figure out ways to make it easy for them. For example, consider expanding the contact page on your website to include every employee in sales and service that a customer would normally work with—and include their email address and phone numbers.

Cease and Desist Customer Runaround

Who owns the customer at your company? If you aren't sure, then you need to rethink the entire process of how you deal with the integration of your sales, service, and support staff. Always assume the customer has both a legitimate issue that needs attention and that her time is more valuable than yours. It is.

Admit When You Are Wrong

We are all human. Surprise, but that means no one is perfect. Customers may not like it, but they understand it. Play it straight and tell them the truth when you screw up. It is a sign of respect they will long remember.

Teach People on the Front Line to Listen

Do you teach deep listening skills? You must. People on the front line in your company should view listening to customers as job one. Profiting from the Power of Me requires hearing both what customers are saying and what they likely mean. Don't confuse the two. For example, irate customers can be set off by something extremely minor that they interpret as a sign of disrespect. Rather than focusing on what they are trying to accomplish, they overreact and take their frustrations out on employees. Employees need to be taught skills that allow them to get to the root of the problem, such as how to ask questions that identify customers' core issues.

Stop Overpromising

Just because your competitor promises something doesn't mean you have to do it too. I know a large residential air conditioning company that decided to promise one-hour service dispatch just because its competitors did. Unfortunately, there was no operational plan in place to deliver on the promise. It just sounded like a good idea to the boss because he was tired of hearing his competitors' radio commercials on the commute to the office. Customers are smart; they know a marketing gimmick when they see it. I guarantee that knee-jerk promises will do much more harm than good.

The Power of Me Means Partnership

The Power of Me is no more complicated than understanding that people want and deserve respect. Companies that continue to disrespect their customers will eventually lose them to thriving Customer CEO competitors. Customer CEO companies understand that they are in a partnership with their customers to accomplish what the customer needs. As you engage customers by treating them with sincere respect, you will profit by creating a higher level of trust than your competitors enjoy. For some, this requires a hard turn in attitudes about your customers. But it should be clear that this transformation is critical. I would submit that the companies that get this right would earn the undying loyalty of Jerry, Elaine, George, and Kramer by recognizing them each as individuals, as selfish as they might be. Just imagine the possibilities if George Constanza became your biggest fan. Wonders never cease with the Power of Me.

(How well does your organization engage the Power of Me? Visit customerceopowercheck.com to download our free diagnostic tool.)

4

The Power of Value

What's this worth to me?

Rock and Roll Hall of Famer David Lee Roth, of Van Halen fame, spoke for a lot of us when he said, "Money can't buy happiness, but it can buy a huge yacht that sails right next to it."[1] Some of us would settle for a two-person bass boat. Or maybe just a float for the swimming pool. Value, it seems, is relative. Only rock stars have yachts.

When we ponder the idea of what something's worth, it is hard to put our finger on it. Value is something different for each person, isn't it? Why does one person not care about the kind of cell phone he talks on, while another will stand in line several days and nights to be among the first to possess the latest iPhone version? Everyone marches to the beat of her own drummer when it comes to the subject of value.

In my firm's research over the years, we have constantly probed customers about how they determine the value of particular products and services. A man named Eldon, who we interviewed in Los Angeles, actually quoted David Lee Roth to explain his viewpoint. Eldon already seemed happy the evening we met him, but he indicated he would be even happier when he too took delivery of a yacht someday. I'm willing to bet Elroy is still dreaming of blue skies, deep water, and the spray of saltwater on his face.

$8 a Bottle

A well-known and highly viewed segment from comedic team Penn & Teller's Showtime program looked at the subject of value through the lens of water.[2] It seems that many Americans prefer bottled water to plain old tap water. As one woman interviewed for the show said, "You know, it's not as impure as tap water can be. Some of the tap water I really don't trust."[3] So the comedic duo put water to the value test. With hidden cameras, they filmed upscale diners making their way to the world's first boutique vendor of…bottled water. Stewards extolled the various virtues of the aqua refreshments, some selling for as much as $8 per bottle. Sadly, the joke was on the unsuspecting aficionados, who were imbibing water that came from a garden hose, not from majestic mountain ranges or lush valley streams. It seems customers are willing to pay more for perceived value. Of course, after they learned of the trickery it was probably a long time before they would be fooled again.

In their business strategy book *Blue Ocean Strategy*, W. Chan Kim and Renée Mauborgne lay out an excellent tool they call the Buyer Utility Map to evaluate relative value.[4] (If you haven't read the book, let me assure you it has nothing to do with yachts or rock stars.) It follows the customer journey through six stages of the buying experience. The authors theorize that people also use six levers to evaluate how well a product or service fits their particular needs. Kim and Mauborgne believe that many companies do not deliver exceptional value to customers, in part because companies often become enamored of their own innovations without first determining whether they actually deliver the value customers are seeking.

This Helps Us How?

I am reminded of a very successful and extremely egotistical real estate investor I know who made several fortunes buying and selling apartment buildings. He also fancied himself a technology guru. This man sank over $3 million of his personal wealth into the development of a new web-based price comparison technology he believed would be perfect for young families looking to buy their first home. He was convinced that a subscription-based business model was the only way to go to market.

Unfortunately, he didn't ask any of his future customers what they thought about this idea before spending his money. He had completely relied on his own opinions, that were echoed by a few of his well-paid employees. No one considered it worth the time or energy to talk to potential customers to test the waters before investing the cash. By the time I was asked to look at the problem and interview potential customers, it was too late. Potential customers found the product difficult to understand and the website hard to navigate. At their income level, they weren't willing to subscribe to the service because they would only use it once every few years. More than one couple said, "And this helps us how?" While the investor evaluated the bad news we had to report, the housing market crashed, and suddenly nobody was a prospect. And our real estate tycoon was several million dollars poorer. Oh well, it happens to the nicest guys.

Over the years, we have observed that customers decide what something is worth to them based upon their unique needs at that moment in time. But, and this is key, their needs are now more affected by external events than we have previously seen.

The term "consumer confidence" has a larger halo effect in the current climate because your customers have often gone through some personal economic disruptions of their own over the past few years. A combination of lost jobs, closed malls, and the constant drumbeat of negative news has created a deep sense of uncertainty. The truth is that people are more afraid for their futures than we have seen in our research work since the 1980s.

Two Universal Truths

We have learned that customers have two universal concerns about value; it doesn't matter whether they are male or female, young or old, poor or rich. The first is the fear of paying too much. Customers will always relate personal anecdotes about "getting ripped off." The second concern is the apparently terrifying possibility of dealing with a "fly by night" company. These enterprises must be avoided at all costs. As a Customer CEO company, how should you process this information? How do you prove the worth of your products and services to a skeptical, often cynical, potential customer?

Their perceptions tend to fall into two extremes on an imaginary value continuum. On one end, customers think that "greedy" companies simply charge too much to fatten their evil CEOs' paychecks. On the other end, customers believe there are companies that mystically understand their customers.

These benevolent enterprises are viewed as fair and equitable, regardless of what they charge. In our consulting practice, we have come to refer to this phenomenon as Polarized Price Perception. It is often illogical, but as we have already seen, Customer CEOs don't have to be logical. They are in charge.

Price Check in Aisle Four

Remember in the pre-bar code days when you had to ask a store clerk to check the price of an item because the tag had fallen off?

Now, there's no need for the clerk or the tag. The Internet has opened an entirely new frontier for discovering value. Consider showrooming.[5] That's what happens when a shopper browses the merchandise in a store with zero intent to buy. The shopper's sole interest is scanning a bar code using tools like Amazon's Price Check app to compare online prices. *The Wall Street Journal* reported that a shopper study by research firm ClickIQ found most people would gladly visit their local big box mass merchandiser to do "product research" with the specific intent of buying the item on Amazon.[6] A Pew Research Study reported that an estimated 5 percent of mobile phone customers actually purchased online while in a physical store during the 2011 holiday shopping period.[7] Many retailers are hopping mad and pushing state legislatures to adopt "e-fairness" laws that would try to ban this practice or at least force e-tailers like Amazon to pay state sales tax.

Of course, there are two sides to this story. Longtime retail analysts know this is just retail evolution. In the good old days, long before the Internet, local chains could call the shots. They offered a relatively limited brand selection, charged a fair price, provided good service, and did quite well. Then, catalog retailers jumped into the market and badly disrupted the status quo. They offered steep discounts from faraway warehouses. So shoppers would head over to the local store to try out the product only to return home to call the toll-free number and order the item. The customer demonstrated that the price was much more important, and he didn't want to pay more at the local store for a friendly guy in a blue vest telling him everything he probably didn't even want to know about a product. Next, the big boxes marched in with their superior, predatory buying power and even steeper discounts. The customers flocked in their doors because price was driving everything.

Now the mass merchandisers are in a huff because the worm has turned on them. They didn't shed any tears for the local and regional chains they put out of business. Some are being proactive in response. Nordstrom is offering free shipping for in-store shoppers.[8] Target has gone another step by working with vendors to create exclusive products available only in its stores.[9] The point is, the customer is in the driver's seat and a business model is only as good as the customers who support it.

Warren Buffet said, "Price is what you pay. Value is what you get."[10] To better understand value, always consider four major areas of inquiry as part of the project to help understand the big picture of what's driving value.

- What are today's major societal trends?
- What are the prevailing industry pressures?
- What are the prevailing macroeconomic headwinds?
- What are the prevailing market issues?

If you are already spending quality time listening to your customers, asking the right questions about value will help you explore rich veins of future growth. Let's take a look at some exceptional Customer CEO companies that understand the Power of Value.

We Are with You

In our family, we always drove GM cars and trucks. It was the buy American thing. But my wife and I decided to switch to a Hyundai Sonata last year for the first time. She did all the research online and at first I didn't believe it, but the value was amazing. What a great car. We've probably sold another ten for the dealer by telling our friends how much we love it.

Dan, Birmingham, Alabama
Participant in a focus group about new cars

We can see the Power of Value nowhere more profoundly than in the car-buying experience. The dealer distribution system is part of the fabric of American life. For more than fifty years the men who built Detroit created an almost perfect mousetrap. Ill-informed customers were lured into brightly lit showrooms to see the newest shiny coupes, sedans, trucks, and sports utility vehicles. Then the Internet came along and seemingly changed everything. New brand names like cars.com, carfax.com, and edmunds.com proliferated, with ads extolling the advantages of this new and improved way to buy a car. This was a way where the customer was finally in control, not a slick sales guy in an ugly plaid jacket.

But not so fast. Maybe the Customer CEO is still not very well thought of in this system. According to CNBC anchor Becky Quick, she and her husband decided to take the plunge and buy a new minivan with the impending arrival of their third child. She wrote, "But getting someone to take $40,000 from you can be tougher than you might think as I learned at one Chrysler, one Honda and three Toyota dealerships."[11] And exactly what was the problem? Sexism was alive and well at every dealership. It seemed that wherever Quick and her husband went, the male salesperson ignored her and deferred to her husband, although she was the one making the decision. This made no sense, because women are the primary buyers of 44 percent of vehicles and have significant influence over 80 percent of those bought.[12]

Why would a car dealership allow such ignorance to still exist in their business? It's because too many companies are still stuck in that trophy case I discussed in chapter 1. Perhaps this is a big clue as to why there's one auto brand running laps around its competition. That brand is Hyundai.

In the hugely competitive used car market, no sign could be a bigger compliment than the one that read, "$1,000 extra for your Hyundai!"[13] The compliment was more significant because it was posted in the front showroom window of a competing dealer across the street from a Las Vegas Hyundai dealership. Hyundai Motor America (HMA) has gained a loyal and steadily growing following, like Dan from our focus group. John Krafcik, president and CEO of HMA said, "Our cars research really well and when you finally get in the car and drive it, it stands up to that research."[14]

Of course, in the ultracompetitive global car market, nothing happens by accident. HMA learned a lot about itself by discovering even more about its current and future customers through an ingenious and radical solution: the company decided to talk to them. The purpose was to discover how to design vehicles that better fulfilled new customer needs. The brand needed to develop a new design concept for its second-generation Santa Fe model. The company hoped to use research both to clarify customer needs to its product designers and to help spark creativity. Hyundai was beginning a revolutionary process of transforming the company into a customer-first company. HMA executives Heather Kluter and Doug Mottram explained that this customer-driven approach had never been done before at Hyundai. They created a persona for their target customer. Kluter and Mottram wrote, "We called this target 'Glamour Mom' and screened numerous women to find a handful of true glamour moms who fit the demographic and lifestyle description of this target."[15]

What research technique did the brand use to drive along with its Glamour Mom? The company decided to employ ethnography, which is the official market research term for observation. The marketing team watched how these women lived in their homes and managed life in general, asked plenty of questions, and let the women explain how their lives really worked. The HMA executives explained, "We got to know what mattered to them, so that we could make the Santa Fe more meaningful to them."[16]

In spending time with their target customers, the Hyundai team got a much richer picture of their customers' needs than they could have gained in a one-hour focus group or a telephone survey. This was not a market research project; this was living, breathing, actionable insight that met customers where they lived.

Not content to just design better cars that helped people, Hyundai used its new customer-centric approach to solve a daunting industry problem. In late 2008, when the car market was in free fall, the usual litany of discounts, rebates, and cheap financing was failing to lift the market. Hyundai had to do something fresh that could address its customer problem when and where it counted. Based on new research, Hyundai introduced its

Assurance plan. As the company website explains, "Purchasing a new vehicle is one of life's big events. You want to know everything you can about the true value of your options. But at the time of purchase, how can you know the future trade-in value of the vehicle you are considering?"[17]

With Assurance, the brand removed a large barrier to future value by guaranteeing what the car would be worth in three or four years. This set Hyundai apart from every other brand because the company was becoming partners with its customers, not adversaries.

Dave Zuchowski, Hyundai's head of U.S. sales, explained the appeal of Assurance: "Our intent with Assurance is to provide certainty in uncertain times and give people a safety net. It really struck a cord[sic]. We expected it would set us apart because it was something no one else was doing."[18]

Whether designing an entirely new kind of car or figuring out a way to help people buy it, Hyundai set a high standard for the Power of Value because it joined hands with customers to say, "We are with you." What's that worth?

Bathing in Beads

Everyone thinks our industry is cutting edge. Actually, the opposite is true when it comes to the tools we use in our labs. Some of this equipment was designed a very long time ago. Sometimes I'm amazed we can get our work done. It can be unsafe, inefficient, and even a biohazard. Someone's going to get hurt or sick.
Richard, San Antonio, Texas
Participant in a customer interview about life science laboratory equipment

Billions of dollars are spent by private industry, universities, and government agencies running thousands of laboratory experiments every year. It turns out that the majority of these experiments fail, many for reasons unrelated to the science, including clumsiness and biohazards in the lab. A small group of enterprising entrepreneurs had the foresight to carefully listen to the real problems life scientists experienced in the lab. This future customer insight made it clear that the lab needed protection from itself. Dubbing this new effort Lab Armor, the company made its mantra "Must protect the lab!"

As the Lab Armor team discussed various ways to protect laboratories, they quickly focused on the lowly water bath, a device that had seen virtually no innovation for nearly fifty years. Here are three nonscientific definitions related to this subject. A *water bath* is a device that scientists use to regulate the temperature of various substances they need in their experiments. Think of a rectangular stainless steel tub that holds about two gallons of water. It has a dial on the front to control small heating elements in the tub. The water needs to be heated to the proper working temperature for the various reagents used in experiments. A *reagent* is simply a substance or compound the bench scientist needs to induce a reaction in her experiment. These reagents are heated in bottles, test tubes, and other vials that are held in the water baths by racks or blocks. A *bench scientist* is kind of that mad scientist who stays locked up in a lab conducting hands-on research, sometimes called "wet science."

Through Lab Armor's interviews and observations, the team learned that bench scientists are fairly intense people, highly focused on the task at hand. Unfortunately, this means that accidents happen frequently because the scientists accidentally knock containers over in the water. Water spills on lab floors, creating potential safety hazards. Typical water baths were also extremely energy inefficient. Worst of all, water baths are inherently not eco-friendly because of mold and bacteria that can rapidly multiply and ruin the experiment and potentially harm the user.

The answer was to replace the water with something better, something that was both moisture and gas impermeable. Lab Armor needed a material that had high thermal conductivity with a wide working temperature range. Through a series of experiments, the Lab Armor team developed what they called the first waterless water bath, the "bead bath." Instead of using a liquid, the team used an entirely new medium to heat reagents while holding them firmly in place. Imagine thousands of smooth, rounded, metal beads, like tiny M&Ms, poured into an empty bath in the place of water. But these new Lab Armor beads cost money. They weren't free, like H_2O.

The key business question was whether labs would buy something (beads) that had previously been free (water). Landon Wood, Lab Armor cofounder, explained that, "Our value challenge was to illustrate that the status quo of using water was costing every lab a lot of money. Sure, water seems free, but when we ran the numbers for lost experiments and ruined production runs from water bath contamination and the labor costs of warming up and cleaning the baths, it was clear that we had a winner."[19]

The market response was overwhelming, because Lab Armor had listened to customers on the front lines. The company translated a series of long-standing pain points into gain. It had solved multiple problems in one simple execution. One scientist at Vanderbilt University commented, "Purchased to decrease water bath contamination. Experience has been wonderful with decreased time taken for cleaning and decreased contamination of tissue culture."[20]

This new bead technology saves time, stays clean, helps a lab be more organized, and is eco-friendly. The firm has gone on to create a series of other lab-related products, including the first bead bath that optimizes bead performance. Lab Armor's products are being used in thousands of life science labs around the world. Most importantly, the Lab Armor story illustrates why ignoring the customer is foolhardy. Let's be clear about what happened here: the customer did not invent the bead technology. But scientists had a series of problems that no one had ever taken the time to observe or really think about. The Lab Armor team had the fresh eyes and ears to listen and clearly observe the problems in the lab, and they were able to create a more valuable product and user experience for their customers.

Big Box of Bargains

It seems to me that no matter how I try to plan it, my food costs keep going up. They say inflation is flat, but I don't believe it. How do I find any real value anymore? With our family of five, I may have to put the kids to work to pay for their food!
Elizabeth, Columbia, South Carolina
Participant in a focus group about grocery stores

Elizabeth spoke for many customers we have interviewed over the past few years. I have met hundreds of people like Elizabeth, and I like to refer to these customers as "momconomists." These moms, whether married or single, have a gnawing feeling that no matter what kind of money-saving strategy they put in place, the deck is stacked against them. Between escalating prices for gas, food, and insurance, the lack of value is a front-burner issue. They know their dollar doesn't go as far as it did last month or last year.

I wasn't surprised to hear Elizabeth explain how she had become an active user of manufacturers' coupons. Our research has shown that conventional wisdom is wrong, as it so often is, with regard to who actually uses coupons. Coupon use typically makes a strong comeback during recessions, particularly with more affluent and educated customers like Elizabeth. She explained to us that in some cases, stores will allow a customer to redeem a $3 coupon for an item that only costs $2. They then allow customers to apply the leftover dollar to noncoupon items like produce or milk. Elizabeth also pointed out that coupons are more plentiful and easier to use these days, thanks to brands' use of social media. For example, she described how she now gets great coupons by "liking" a specific brand on Facebook.

During this South Carolina focus group session, something unexpected happened when another woman, named Lucy, asked Elizabeth why she didn't shop at Costco. Lucy was a self-described Costco addict. She told us, "Every week, I buy almost all my groceries and household supplies there. I have the executive membership so I get 2 percent back. I use a Costco Amex card so that's worth another 1 percent. And for every $2500 I spend I get $50 back. I also get 3 percent back on gas. Forget those damn coupons, look how much money you will save!"

It turns out that every day, more than three million people like Lucy enter the doors of one of Costco Wholesale's six hundred stores. The company's sales are approaching $90 billion annually.[21] It's a bare-bones operation, with a warehouse look and feel. The company saves on fixtures, lighting, and décor. Most people come for the value because Costco marks up nationally known brands a maximum of 14 percent. It limits its "own" brand markup to 15 percent. Supermarkets aim for a 25 percent markup; department stores shoot for 50 percent.[22] Costco cofounder and former CEO Jim Sinegal told the *New York Times*, "We're very good merchants, and we offer value.... The traditional retailer will say: 'I'm selling this for $10. I wonder whether I can get $10.50 or $11.' We say: 'We're selling it for $9. How do we get it down to $8?'"[23]

Once Lucy spoke up at the focus group, the Costco fans jumped on the bandwagon. Sixty percent of the women we interviewed were regular Costco shoppers. Although we were not there specifically to discuss Costco, I want to share some of the comments we heard, to underscore how Costco embraces the Power of Value. It's compelling.

Focus group member Barbara said, "The problem with Costco is that the deals are so good I buy stuff I don't really need. If you can just look and not buy, shopping there is a ton of fun."

Marge told us, "The Costco pharmacy is a lifesaver. Walgreen's was going to charge me $430 for one of my prescriptions. I tried Costco and their generic brand was only $50. Plus I get 2 percent cash back from my Costco card."

Linda explained that saving money was critical but that she loves "that they know me by name when I go there. Maybe that means I go there too much!"

What Lexie told us should be a threat to traditional grocery chains. "My husband and I quit going to the regular grocery and department stores years ago. I don't know how they stay in business. Everyone I know goes to Costco. And their Kirkland wine is fantastic! At $6.99, it's a steal!"

Marge later explained, "To be honest, shopping at Costco is an adventure. I always find something new and it's always at a fantastic price. My friend is a buyer for a grocery store and he told me Costco never marks anything up more than 14 percent. It shows. They won me over. Fun and cheap is a good combination."

Lucy whispered to the other women about what to look for, like it was a state secret: "One secret I have learned is that anything they are closing out ends in .88. I read about it on a web forum. It's true."

These focus groups showed us again that it is not unusual for Customer CEO companies like Costco to have their own urban legends. Several other comments, which we couldn't confirm, were about secret signage and mystery merchandise. These are all part of what happens when a company creates a cult following. Pretty good for a major retail brand that doesn't advertise, charges an annual membership fee to shop in its stores, and only offers about four thousand items. To compare, Walmart stores usually offer a hundred thousand products.

But being a Customer CEO company goes even deeper. Costco cuts costs everywhere in order to maximize value for customers. To reduce electricity costs, the company uses skylights in its stores, which cuts back on lighting on sunny days. And what other Fortune 500 company have you heard of where executives— including the CEO—answer their own phones? Costco loves the Power of Value, but you haven't seen anything yet. It is possible to offer so much value that you turn your company into another kind of cult. Let's fly Ryanair.

The Airline Customers Love to Hate

Customer: When I was in Dublin last year for six months, I flew Ryanair almost every week to other cities in Europe. I hate Ryanair with a passion. I hope they never set up shop in America.

Interviewer: Why did you keep flying them if you hated them so much?
Customer: Because they are almost free. If you are willing to put up with their BS for a couple of hours, it's worth it. Just grin and bear it.

Scott, Dallas, Texas
Participant in customer interview about airlines

I was intrigued when I met Scott because he was so passionate about this airline. It turns out Scott wasn't alone. Ryanair is so reviled that there are websites and blogs dedicated to how much current and former customers hate them. Here's a typical entry from one site called ihateryanair.org.

A stewardess from Ryanair, the World's most hated airline, was injured on Tuesday after falling from the rear door of the aircraft onto the floor some 3 meters below. It is yet unknown whether she fell accidently, jumped or was pushed by a disgruntled passenger.[24]

According to the Swedish news site *The Local*, this incident actually happened on May 8, 2012, at the Gothenburg City Airport in Sweden. The site reported that, "An air hostess fell out of an aircraft exit at the Gothenburg City Airport on Tuesday and was brought to hospital, bleeding from the head."[25] The airport CEO, Annika Nyberg, told the press that she had never seen anything like it in her career. Of course, the blogger added his editorial spin. What has Ryanair done to deserve this much hate?

Ryanair was a tiny, money-losing Irish airline until Michael O'Leary showed up. After traveling to Dallas in the early 1990s to look at the Southwest Airlines model, the new CEO decided that a low-fare strategy was the ticket for Ryanair. Initially, he followed much of the Southwest formula: flying to small, out-of-the-way airports (routes often called "nowhere to nowhere"), operating a single type of plane, short hauls, no reserved seating, and incredibly cheap fares.

Now the airline is the largest in Europe, with more than 1,300 daily departures from twenty-six countries. They can get you to more than 150 different cities on their fleet of 250 Boeing 737s. Nearly seventy-five million passengers fly Ryanair each year. If Ryanair could be described with one word it would be "cheap." You'd be hard pressed to name another major brand in the world that would want to associate itself with the word cheap. Particularly when the service involves a life or death matter. Conventional wisdom says that the flying public wouldn't want to get on a plane described as cheap. Somewhere in their minds, passengers might wonder, "Will it fly or crash?" But, Ryanair defies the odds on this, as it does on so many other things.

If you want comfort and coddling, Ryanair isn't your airline. Your seat won't recline. There are no pull-down window shades. Or seat pockets. The optional onboard food is expensive. There is an online, per-passenger booking fee. You must print your boarding pass yourself or you will be charged for one at the airport. There are myriad other fees for administration, priority boarding, reserved seating, infants, infant equipment, sports equipment, musical instruments, flight changes, and baggage. On its website, the airline spells out its philosophy: "Here at Ryanair, all of our optional fees are designed to encourage passengers to travel in a low-cost way, which enables Ryanair to save costs and pass on these savings through the lowest possible fares to you and your family."[26] O'Leary told the *New York Times* that he only promises his passengers low fares, a good on-time record, few cancellations, and few lost bags. He said, "But if you want anything more—go away! Will we put you in a hotel room if your flight was canceled?" Mr. O'Leary asked rhetorically. "No! Go away."[27]

Having never personally flown the airline, I decided to line up a few interviews with Ryanair customers via Skype. Richard in Belfast told me that he couldn't understand the European media obsession with the airline. "Look, you don't have to fly them.

There are plenty of other carriers to get you there. But, you will pay more. Usually a lot more."

Anna, a fashion designer who resides in London, explained that O'Leary is "a lightning rod. He is a modern P.T. Barnum and wants to draw the attention he gets. I view him as the anti-Richard Branson, the CEO of Virgin Air. You rarely read any negative press about Branson because he plays to the media. O'Leary wants to wear the black hat to get a huge amount of free press. You're writing about him in your book, right?"

I asked each of my interviewees how much they have personally saved on Ryanair. The consensus was a discount in the range of 75 percent over traditional, full-fare carriers. In some cases, the savings can be even greater.

John, a business consultant based in Dublin, explained, "We like to call it 'the sit down and shut up airline.' As long as you are willing to be one of the cows in the cattle car, it's cool. I probably used them about ten times last year. There's only so much you can take. But to be honest, I really admire O'Leary. You always know where you stand. Literally."

John was referring to Ryanair's most infamous stunt. In 2011, O'Leary announced a plan to sell standing space for about $6 per flight. He planned to remove ten rows of seats and replace them with fifteen rows of what he called "vertical seating." Standing passengers would be held in place by a shoulder belt. Of course, the media went crazy with dozens of stories about the profit-obsessed O'Leary. The European Aviation Safety Agency announced that the idea was "unprecedented and highly unlikely to be certified in the near future."[28] Plane manufacturer Boeing said in a statement, "We are not considering standing-only accommodations. Stringent regulatory requirements—including seats capable of withstanding a force of 16 times gravity—pretty much preclude such an arrangement."[29]

We asked Thomas, a director of sales in the automotive industry who frequently flies throughout Europe, what he thought of standing-room seating: "This is akin to selling a car without a windshield. You might get there, but in what kind of shape?"

Is Ryanair a Customer CEO company? It all depends on your point of view. Michael O'Leary clearly wants to be loved by his shareholders, and if he upsets the flying public and the media in the process, he isn't concerned. It is undeniable that he provides extreme value to his customers. Even his worst critics agree that the cheap seats are a significant value. In this case, Customer CEOs may grumble and complain, but they are still in charge of the final decision about how much money they wish to save. Can seventy-five million of them be wrong?

How to Profit from the Power of Value

The clear profit from creating Customer CEO value is growth. Any company can dig in to learn what its products and services are worth to its customers. This chapter has reviewed some extremes, from Lab Armor, which created something out of nothing by replacing free water with beads, to Ryanair, which charges almost nothing but still delivers a traveler's most important desire, a safe trip.

At the heart of the Power of Value is customer satisfaction. Customers will evaluate your product or service brands by asking themselves four major questions. First, what is the overall quality of your offering? Second, are your "points of contact," whether in store, online, or contact centers, fully integrated for ease of use, information gathering, and follow up after the sale? Third, does your offering match the price point you are asking? Fourth, is the overall experience you provide worth it?

Economic uncertainty says all bets are off when it comes to our past perceptions about and experiences with customers. Short-term recessions usually don't require structural changes. However, current global conditions do not reflect a short-term problem. Because the downturn has lingered for as many years as it has, customer perceptions about value ("What's this worth to me?") have changed. Your knowledge is outdated. What can you do about it? Seize the opportunity to love the Power of Value.

Think of Yourself As Chief Growth Officer

Begin to introduce the idea of behavioral segmentation, much like Hyundai did. Simply put, design ways for customers to do business with you. Every shift in the market is a new opportunity to grow your base by winning over new customers. You must forget what you learned last year, or worse, five years ago. That information is no longer valid, regardless of how good your sales currently are.

Listen to Customers' Ideas About Value

When you talk to customers or conduct research involving them, focus on open-ended questions so you will be in a position to capture the nuggets. That's where the insight really is. Learn how the current economy is affecting your customers. It is critical you understand how their purchasing decisions have changed. What are their barriers to buying? Learn how your products stack up. Ask what it would take for them to see your offerings in a better light. Remember that every day your firm is not actively engaged in listening is an opportunity for your competitors. That's just a fact.

Here's the secret of the Power of Value: you don't have to guess what people are willing to pay for your products or services. There are four critical questions you need to ask. Know that when you ask people directly about price, they will almost always say it is too high. You have to approach the subject as if you are conducting a customer satisfaction survey. I have found that people are rarely asked about their attitudes toward pricing, and they are usually glad to engage.

- Ask customers how many other products or services they considered before selecting yours. If they picked yours without looking at other options, you probably left money on the table. If they selected you over several competitors, you are well priced.

- Find out if they believe the value they received equals the price they paid.
- If they feel that there should be greater value, probe deeper to uncover what additional features they would like.
- On the other hand, it is just as important to learn which features are unimportant to them. This is valuable insight because it can lead to eliminating what I like to call "dinosaur costs," features that were once important but are no longer needed.

After You've Listened, Look for the Gaps

Every product or service needs periodic overhaul because customer needs almost invariably change over time. For example, Hyundai gained fresh insight from its customer study about designing car interiors, a study that was inspired by model homes in the neighborhoods of their "Glamour Moms." These customers clearly preferred the warm wood and color palettes used throughout the model homes. Hyundai designers were inspired to add more aesthetically pleasing wood in the new Santa Fe model interiors than they had previously used. Without stepping directly into customers' lives, Hyundai never would have observed this gap, much less been able to fill it. Ultimately, your job as a company is to fill the open gaps. Dive into the gaps to figure out how to close them.

The Power of Value Never Sleeps

Customers never stop seeking value in every transaction and relationship. Be vigilant by proactively engaging your customers and discovering new ways to satisfy them.

(How well does your organization engage the Power of Value? Visit customerceopowercheck.com to download our free diagnostic tool.)

5

The Power of Performance

Does this do the job
I need it to do?

Things either work or they don't. For customers, there really is no middle ground. The question is why there are so many products that don't work.

In theory, it seems simple enough. The Baldrige Performance Excellence Program is dedicated to improve the competitiveness and performance of U.S. organizations. It defines product performance as "performance relative to measures and indicators of product and service characteristics important to customers. Examples include product reliability, on-time delivery, customer-experienced defect levels, and service response time."[1]

Yet, most experts agree that more than 90 percent of new products fail. Sometimes the product is poorly marketed. Other times, it is a brand extension that is so far afield of the root brand that potential buyers are confused. But usually it is because the product doesn't do what the customer needs it to do in the first place.

Fail

There's a place where products that just didn't perform end up. It's kind of a graveyard for product flops. Aptly called The Museum of Failed Products, in Ann Arbor, Michigan, the museum houses thousands of losers, many from some of the biggest enterprises in the world. Writer Oliver Burkeman explains why he believes so many failed products line the shelves at the museum:

> Each one must have made it through a series of meetings at which nobody realized that the product was doomed. Perhaps nobody wanted to contemplate the prospect of failure; perhaps someone did, but didn't want to bring it up for discussion. Even if they realize where things are headed, there's a perverse incentive for marketers to plough more money into a lemon: that way, they can force some sales and preserve their dignity. By the time the truth becomes obvious, the original developers will have moved to other products, or other firms. Little energy will have been invested in discovering what went wrong; everyone involved will have conspired, perhaps without realizing what they're doing, never to speak of it again.[2]

It seems that many of these products made it through the company R&D pipeline with little thought, much less consultation with actual potential customers. Who could forget classic brand mash-ups like Ben-Gay aspirin? Clairol's Touch of Yogurt shampoo? Coors Rocky Mountain spring water? Bic underwear? In hindsight, these are colossally bad, even foolish, ideas for products. Is the idea of shampooing with yogurt any better than something called Shell Oil cologne? (To my knowledge, no such product exists.) Thankfully, the marketplace put these pathetic products out of their misery without much fanfare. Here are some other classics from the museum you might remember.

- **Microsoft's Zune:** First released in November 2006, Microsoft thought it had the winning hand to stop the iPod revolution. While it had some nifty product features, the Zune was a bust. It lacked simplicity and style. But the key problem was its lack of performance with the iTunes platform for digital downloads. Apple had created a virtually impenetrable fortress for the music experience, and Microsoft couldn't scale the walls no matter how much money it threw at the market.[3]
- **Colgate Kitchen Entrees:** What a perfectly delightful combination, toothpaste and dinner! Some geniuses at Colgate-Palmolive decided the world needed yet another line of frozen meals. Kitchen Entrees set a new low for brand extensions. The product was a complete disaster because customers could see no valid connection.[4]
- **iSmell:** Imagine a computer-peripheral device designed to dispense aromas for websites you might click on or even e-mails you might open. This terrible product idea made no sense because customers did not desire a smell-fest tied to the web. It just didn't compute. *PC World* magazine pronounced it one of the world's twenty-five worst tech products ever created.[5]

How Does This Happen?

What drove management forward on these incredibly bad product ideas? Were they dreamed up in some kind of stream-of-consciousness brainstorming session? Someone in authority had to approve the idea, then fork out the money for testing, prototyping, production, and marketing. How does this happen?

In his book *Sketching User Experience*, designer Bill Buxton writes, "Hardly a day goes by that we don't see an announcement for some new product or technology that is going to make our lives easier, solve some or all of our problems, or simply make the world a better place. Few of these products survive, much less deliver on their typically over-hyped promise."[6]

Buxton and great designers like him believe that there is no design context. "To design a tool, we must understand the larger physical, social, and psychological context in which it will be used. And that's something designers are trained to do," Buxton says.[7]

This means simply that when companies ignore the human side of product performance they are setting themselves up for failure. Customer-focused design is the key to performance. What's the point of creating bizarre new product combinations or adding bells and whistles if the ultimate buyer doesn't care about them? If customers are happy with the products they are currently using, it's doubtful they will suddenly feel compelled to switch to a new product. In fact, most companies, even conservative ones, wildly overestimate the success their new offering will have in the market. Harvard Business School professor John Gourville explained the fundamental problem as sellers overvaluing their new product by a factor of three. At the same time, new customers are often reluctant to part with their incumbent product, and overvalue it by an additional factor of three. Gourville's theory is that this condition results in new products being overvalued by a factor of nine, or what he calls The 9x Effect.[8]

It's clear that companies need to have a clearer path to understanding the performance criteria their customers expect. Better design must be present in products, services, and experiences, and we must rethink how we approach design to satisfy the Power of Performance. Let's take a look at some examples of companies that understand this.

Tear Down the Walls

I scheduled an appointment at the Apple Store's Genius Bar to get my iMac checked out. But I ended up leaving with a brand new iPad. Now I know why Apple calls it the "Genius Bar."

Ivan, Phoenix, Arizona
Participant in a focus group about retail stores

Gensler, the global architectural, design, planning, and consulting firm, conducts regular workplace surveys. The firm has identified the importance of designing work spaces that encourage people to collaborate, learn, and socialize. One of Gensler's key precepts is to remove barriers that restrict these activities.[9] Put another way, today's best work spaces hardly resemble the closed-off, symmetrical, walnut-paneled offices of the 1960s we see in television series like *Mad Men*.

From a Customer CEO point of view, we can clearly see that tearing down barriers between employees and customers can be transformative and unbelievably profitable. All we have to do is look at what Apple has done with its stores, which produce seventeen times more in sales per square foot than the national retail average.[10]

Ron Johnson, former senior vice president of retail operations at Apple, now CEO of J.C. Penney Company, told a Fortune Brainstorm Tech Conference in Aspen that "Apple has always offered the most easy out-of-the-box user experience, but we noticed there was a gap between buying and using. Even the easiest product set-up intimidated people. So we said, if we can set up a product for them in the ten minutes before they left the store and they started using it and falling in love with it, it would be transformational. It was an insight that made the Apple Store relevant."[11]

According to retail market analytics firm Asymco, Apple produced $5,626 per square foot as of August 2011.[12] That was twice the amount generated by the number-two retailer, exclusive high-end jeweler Tiffany & Co. To put this staggering number in perspective, most analysts consider $300 per square foot to be good. This success begs the question, why isn't everyone doing what Apple does?

Obviously, other companies don't necessarily have the products or cult following of the Apple brand. But there is something else going on in the Apple Store that's truly different, and that captures the Customer CEO Power of Performance. I believe it is a combination of a unique layout and a unique way of interacting with customers.

What do you notice the moment you walk into an Apple Store? There are no walls and no sales counters. Your line of sight is not obstructed in any way as you gaze into the approximately eight-thousand-square-foot space. Apple has torn down both the physical and psychological walls that separate customer and employee.

As the Gensler study encouraged, Apple has created a place where collaboration, learning, and socializing can flourish. Every customer, no matter his level of computer literacy, is encouraged to play with the equipment. There is something compelling about standing beside an Apple sales associate who is demonstrating the newest MacBook Pro rather than facing her over the barrier of a counter. This gesture says, "We're working through this together" to a customer. This is a decided advantage and shows why Ivan, our focus group commenter, is not an exception at Apple but the rule.

Of course, none of this is an accident. I interviewed two former Apple sales associates and they explained that the company has an unorthodox attitude about "not selling, but helping customers." They talked about how associates were taught a five-step customer-facing process, using APPLE as an acronym:

- Approach the customer with a personalized warm welcome.
- Probe politely to understand what the customer needs.

- Present a solution for the customer to take home today.
- Listen for and resolve any issues or concerns.
- End with a fond farewell and an invitation to return.

Apple doesn't stop there. The associate offers you a simple check-out. No need for a shopping basket or to stand in line at a cash register so they can sell you a little tchotchke or a soft drink. No, all it takes is one simple swipe of your credit card on the associate's iPhone. You are the proud owner of a new Apple product with a completely paperless transaction and a receipt e-mailed to you while you are standing there. The Genius Bar that Ivan visited to fix his computer often results in no sale. But the service builds value for every Apple user, who sees that the company is serious about satisfying its customers.

What has escaped most experts who love to continue the myth that some visionaries don't do customer research around innovation is that the Apple Stores are, in fact, a real-time, living, breathing customer laboratory. Every transaction and conversation is a listening opportunity that the company leverages to its competitive advantage. Jobs understood this. During a "fireside chat" at the 1997 Apple Worldwide Developers Conference (WWDC) he said, "You've got to start with the customer experience and work back to the technology—not the other way around. I've probably made this mistake more than anybody, and I've got the scar tissue to prove it."[13]

It's important to understand Apple's almost unique obsession with its customers. The company wants not only to super-serve them to keep them coming back, but to continue pushing the boundaries. Based on an analysis of Apple's balance sheet, the company invests a whopping $10 million per store.[14] That's about $1,250 per square foot. On the other hand, according to Reed Construction Data, traditional retailers usually invest less than $2 million for a new eight-thousand-square-foot store.[15] No doubt, it's expensive to be Apple.

Germaphobe's Paradise

*If they really want me as their customer, why are their bathrooms
so disgusting? I mean what in world are they thinking? Their
little ad campaign shows all these smiling faces, but none of them
obviously set foot in one of those stalls. I will never go back.*

Marlene, Flower Mound, Texas
Participant in a focus group about grocery store chains

Ask a woman about unclean bathrooms and the reactions range
from mild indignation to outrage. I know because I have heard
about this delicate subject for more than twenty years. If I were
building any kind of retail establishment, I would dramatically
increase the budget to design high-performance bathrooms.
Then I would allocate even more money to maintain them every
hour of every day. Common sense, you say? A clean bathroom,
or the lack thereof, is still the number-one complaint I hear from
female customers, regardless of industry.

In his book *Customers for Life*, auto dealer Carl Sewell
explained the power of the bathroom. "Now, nobody has ever
said to me, 'You know, I bought a car from you because your restrooms are so clean.' But there have been a lot of women who've
told me, 'Your ladies room is beautiful.' "[16] After he hired the
late Stanley Marcus to help him reinvent his dealerships, Sewell
invested heavily in remodeling his bathrooms. It was clear that
bathrooms make a statement.

In that spirit, it shows when a company is willing to take a
deep dive into its toilets and embrace customer attitudes about
dirty bathrooms. I found two firms that are putting bathroom
first and foremost in their business models.

You may have never heard of Buc-ee's, a small, Texas-based
convenience store chain with fewer than thirty locations. But the
chain has developed a fanatical following, primarily because of its
big, bold, uber-clean, artwork-laden, innovative bathrooms.

If you have ever traveled the interstate highways of America, nature eventually calls. Seedy truck stops, gas stations, and convenience stores usually dot the landscape. Buc-ee's made a strategic business decision early on to not only have the best bathrooms, but to use them as the main draw for the traveling public.

I visited the Buc-ee's store in New Braunfels, Texas, between Austin and San Antonio, and was amazed to enter a store so pristine that I thought I might have walked into an upscale hotel by mistake. The sixty-seven-thousand-square-foot store sits on eighteen acres filled with sixty gas pumps. This facility cost $7.5 million, and there was hardly an empty parking space in the large lot. In addition to the usual convenience store fare of snacks and drinks, Buc-ee's features fresh barbecue, jerky, tacos, and other fresh food. There's an entire section overflowing with kitschy, Texas-themed merchandise, clothing, and outdoor equipment. While I was there, someone announced, "Free fudge!" and the crowd surged toward the candy counter.

And then there are the bathrooms. After walking down a wide and well-lit hallway, you enter a porcelain palace of fully enclosed stalls. By my count there were forty-plus urinals. Open 24–7, the bathrooms are ready for high numbers of people, with Purell dispensers near every urinal. Every stall was like an individual room featuring automatic flushing toilets and seat cleaners. These bathrooms are a perfect germaphobe's paradise and virtually odor free. Of course, they had the obligatory automatic sinks and paper tower dispensers. While I was there, I watched what appeared to be a full-time cleaning crew working their way around the place. The company has used the stores' bathrooms as the major message in their marketing. Billboards across Texas proclaim, "Only 262 miles to Buc-ee's. You can hold it." Or, "Your Throne Awaits." The general manager of the New Braunfels location said, "This is just another step in Buc-ee's quest to take over the world, one clean restroom at a time."[17]

It turns out that bacteria-free bathrooms are big business. Booz & Company conducted a study of the hotel industry and found that customers want cleanliness more than customer service and style.[18] Best Western, with more than twenty-four hundred hotels across America, decided that better performance in the area of cleanliness could be a strong differentiator. The hotel chain hired leading design firm IDEO to gain customer insights for the mid-scale hotel market segment. The results helped the chain adopt the most advanced cleaning technologies, including black lights to locate disgusting biological matter and ultraviolet light wands to destroy it. As *USA Today* reported, travelers have become germ obsessed. "It used to be that you walked into a guest room and saw a stain on the carpet, you'd think the room's dirty," Ron Pohl, a Best Western VP said. "Today, guests don't see any stains, but they still question how clean the room is."[19] In the first months of the new initiative, Best Western's Guest Satisfaction Survey scores for hotels trained to use the new tools were up by double digits.

A Bathtub Full of Dirt

Is there anything filthier than trying to change a vacuum cleaner bag? Pardon the pun, but it really sucks.

Julie, Columbus, Ohio
Participant in a focus group about household appliances

Every home has at least one bathtub. The average tub holds somewhere between 100 and 150 gallons of water. Now, imagine if that tub was filled with dirt. Yes, filthy, grimy, gritty dirt. That's the amount that gets tracked in or blown in through cracks in your doors and windows every year. Of course, that's the thing about dirt. It's really kind of stealth. It sneaks up on you, a little bit at a time. Sometimes you can't see it, but you always know it's there. No matter what kind of preventive measures you might put in place, it keeps coming back 24–7.

That brings us back to the typical vacuum cleaner. It conceals the dirt in an expandable bag. You think the dirt's been captured, but you really aren't sure until you change it. But when you change it, wow, what a mess. As with most problems, it's simple to see, but complicated to solve.

Entrepreneur James Dyson solved the bag problem. It only took 5,271 attempts to get it right. Dyson vacuum cleaners show the dirt other vacuum cleaners hide. Dyson told *Wired* magazine, "We look at something that has a problem...then we develop a technology."[20]

Dyson is a different kind of Customer CEO company. It works on solving long-standing customer pain points before creating the product. James Dyson used the trial-and-error method made famous by Thomas Edison, creating 5,271 prototypes before he was ready to introduce his vacuum cleaner to the marketplace.[21] He believed that most existing upright or canister types did a poor job of sucking up dirt and were a mess to clean out. In a process sometimes called "constructive discontent," problems are solved because a creative person sees a need for improvement and then proposes a solution. James Dyson is one such creative individual.

The problem is that suction power is reduced because dust, pet hair, and dirt clog bags and filters. Dyson's invention relies on what he calls the "cyclonic action of centrifugal force." With no bag to get in the way, Dyson vacuums can keep performing at maximum power. "They maintain constant maximum suction," he says. "All the time it's working to full efficiency, cleaning your home."[22]

This meant Dyson wanted the customer to have visual proof that the technology did what it said it would do. He wanted customers to see the dirt disappear as it filled the vacuum's clear plastic body. This would be proof of his invention's superior simplicity. He knew people didn't like the idea of an expanding bag full of dirt that couldn't be seen. In the beginning, Dyson faced reluctance from retailers, who told him he would never be able to sell a vacuum cleaner where the dirt was visible. Of course, tradition-bound vacuum sellers had another motive; they believed that bags were the gift that kept on giving. They were used to a customer who had to return to the store to buy more bags. Their waiting salespeople could then sell them a slightly new and improved version of the same old vacuum cleaner.

The dealers asked Dyson to do some market research. He reluctantly complied and found that they were right; most people didn't want to see the dirt, they just wanted it to go away. But Dyson has always known his job was to be the innovator. "You can't base a new project two years ahead on current market trends and what users are thinking at the moment. That sounds very arrogant. But it isn't arrogance. You can't go and ask your customers to be your inventors. That's your job."[23]

Dyson believes the most important connection to customers is careful observation of their real world. His innovative solutions have come from having the technical ability to bridge the gap between customer need ("clean floors") and a marketable product. Dyson understands how important the Power of Performance is to his customers, and he will continue to test, fine-tune, and lead. That's the very definition of performance.

Profiting from the Power of Performance

The Power of Performance is, at its heart, driven by better product, service, and experience design. Customer CEO companies recognize that good design is good business. The trick is determining how to create what your customers need at a price point that works for both you and them. Even when customers base their decisions on emotion, they still ask the basic question: Does it do the job I need done? Performance-enhancing features that don't answer that central question are a waste of resources, and won't work in the long run. Every company must decide which strategy works best for its brand but, in the end, the question remains the same: What job needs to be performed?

The Power of Performance is about superior customer engagement through superior design. Apple tore down barriers with better-designed stores, creating a more meaningful experience between customers and employees. Buc-ee's took an old business model—the roadside store—and reinvented it around better-performing bathrooms. Best Western decided to use technology to completely change its brand by giving customers a renewed confidence that their rooms will be cleaner. Dyson designed a better vacuum than the competition. While no one wanted to see the dirt, his solution gave visual evidence of higher performance.

Roger Martin, dean of Rotman School of Management at the University of Toronto, famously said, "Businesspeople don't need to understand designers better; they need to become designers."[24] Design is really imaging that which does not exist. You must stay focused on the big picture, not just the numbers. Great business ideas die in two primary ways: death by silo and death by numbers. In death by silo, the corporate team often contains "devil's advocates," who drop in from their lofty perches in the silo, division, or department. They tend to be the ones who talk about the way things have always been done and why their particular department just can't see the end game. In death by numbers, it is the accountants and bean counters who immediately shoot down the big picture idea as unaffordable on its face. Better design requires a champion (preferably the CEO) to have the best chance of working.

I believe the right way to reframe your thinking around the idea of performance is to start with a big idea: *focus on designing superior customer experiences, no matter what kind of business you are in.* As I reflect on my years of interviewing customers, it is clear that the *experience delivered* has almost always trumped product features. Gadgets may be fun but the experience is what people remember most. It's what they will keep coming back for.

Industrial designer Robert Brunner developed Apple's first MacIntosh PowerBook and many other iconic products during his career. In his book with coauthor Stewart Emery, *Do You Matter? How Great Design Will Make People Love Your Company,* he explained his approach this way:

What this means is to always consider the human element as primary. And within this to recognize the emotional impact of what you are offering. This seems obvious, but it is difficult because of a common paradox: In business we tend to shy away from most things emotional. We'd prefer to rationalize, measure, process and systematize. Ironically, we tend to put faith in things that are decidedly not humanistic: Science. Math. Machines. When the going gets gray, we spring for black and white. But to be great at design, you need to embrace the human condition and recognize that when it's all said and done, this is what will serve you the best. Getting back to that universal question of what do we all want from life, you need to understand that the experience we have of the things and places we spend our time with must be compelling. We want things that are engaging, fun, personal, useful, productive, and desirable. And emotionally rewarding.[25]

When a Customer CEO company truly connects with its customers through the Power of Performance, it profits from a kind of adulation or cultlike status. Adulation isn't a word usually used in business, but it simply means "overenthusiastic praise." Just imagine if you had customers who extolled you to everyone they came into contact with. It all begins with design thinking.

(How well does your organization engage the Power of Performance? Visit customerceopowercheck.com to download our free diagnostic tool.)

6

The Power of the Heart

Key Customer CEO Question:

How do you make me feel?

Business is just an eight-letter word meaning rationality. Our products have complex lists of features and specifications to showcase their strengths. Our service contracts offer pages of fine print to protect against every possible contingency. Detailed budgets and flash sales reports have myriad rows and columns to keep us on track every minute, month, and quarter. We construct multilayered silos to operate in. We hire the best and brightest from the most prestigious academies who deliver perfectly symmetrical PowerPoint presentations to prove beyond any doubt just how buttoned up and rational we can be. Yes, we are a logical, linear, list-making, left-brained lot. We are businesspeople.

Let's consider the business brain, shall we? It's located on the left side, and it's all about being analytical and calculating. It's the part of the brain where we think, "Just the facts and figures, ma'am." In business we have been taught that venturing over to the dark side of the right brain might not be very good for our careers. It's a dangerous place for anyone to linger, with all that artsy, creative, and touchy-feely stuff going on. It's too risky and radical. So we ignore and suppress it. If we wander off the reservation and start to daydream a little with "what if" questions, a giant business magnet in our head immediately brings us back to the "what is." It is safer to stay away from the things that won't fit in a box, neatly tied up with a bow.

But wait a minute. In our annual strategic planning sessions and conferences, prominent facilitators and renowned speakers tell us that we must strive to create raving fans. Our salespeople should become more understanding. The service team needs to wow everyone 24–7. But this advice often goes in one ear and out the other because it is rooted in the right brain. We don't really hear those words of advice because, as strange as it may sound, they are all about love. And love, well, that's complicated. It's the strongest human emotion. We chase it. Get depressed over it. Lie for it. Some of us even kill for it. Others never find it or have a difficult time giving and receiving it. Love might be bliss but it can stink, too. There are no business charts, spreadsheets, or strategies that can express it. Psychology explains that love is made up of intimacy, commitment, and passion. A person might even love a product, service, experience, company, or brand if he values it highly enough and has an attachment to it.

Should we fall in love with our customers? Do you want them to fall in love with you? Or should it be all business, with nothing really personal? As we learned earlier from Gourville's 9x effect, switching products or companies is not necessarily a rational decision. It is often an emotional one, because customers are usually skeptical about a new product, unable to catch the vision of why they need it and satisfied with what they have now.

On the other hand, companies are usually convinced that their new product works like a charm; they easily see a need for it and view their innovation as the gold standard. If customers are from Venus and companies are from Mars, how can the company make its case to create new customers and retain existing ones?

The company trying to persuade customers has to connect at a deeper emotional level. The Power of the Heart describes the idea that people are more willing than ever to love, or at least strongly prefer, new brands that "get them," as we saw with the Power of Me. To succeed, companies have to dig deeper into that unknown: the right brain.

Everybody's Talking

It used to be more fun to go shopping. Now everyone is in such a rush, the lines are so long, and there are just too may items to choose from. I mean, how many different kinds of wine and toothpaste can you have?

Don, Austin, Texas
Participant in a focus group about grocery stores

A while back, there was a radio ad for Trader Joe's grocery store that made fun of competitors that had installed televisions in order to entertain customers while they were checking out. At Trader Joe's, the commercial said, customers could entertain themselves by just talking to store employees. That hardly scratches the surface of the talking that goes on at a typical Trader Joe's every day.

Upon entering a Trader Joe's (TJ's) store, one of the first things you notice is that complete strangers talk to each other. They speak to one another in an easy way reminiscent of an earlier time in America, when people weren't in such a hurry. I noticed this countercultural ritual taking place in the three Trader Joe's locations I visited in Los Angeles, Oakland, and New York City. I wondered what all the talk was about so I asked a few of them what was going on.

In West Hollywood, Sandra, a personal trainer, said she asked another shopper what he thought of the Kauai coffee blend Trader Joe's carries. This led to a more in-depth discussion about grinding and brew times. She and her new expert coffee acquaintance spent more than ten minutes in deep discussion while sampling the coffee of the day.

In the Union Square store in Manhattan, Derrick, a student at Parsons The New School for Design a few blocks away, was chatting up Reby, a student from NYU, about the pros and cons of the dozen or so peanut butter blends in the store.

In the Oakland College Avenue store, Marian, an IT programmer, was in deep conversation with Barb, a hair stylist who worked in the neighborhood. It was their lunch hour, but rather than rushing to leave the store they lingered, discussing the rising costs of produce and Australian Shiraz.

Mark Gardiner, a marketer and ad agency entrepreneur, went undercover as a worker at Trader Joe's in order to write an e-book, *Build a Brand Like Trader Joe's*. In an interview, he confirmed what I had witnessed. "We live in a world where friendliness—just having a friendly conversation—is more and more at a premium....I realized (when I worked there), oh, that's what people are actually coming here for. Talk about something hiding in plain sight! It's the oldest idea, an idea that predates commerce."[1]

It's all part of the special experience that makes the store one of the most unique in America. Since it gained its identity as Trader Joe's in 1967, the company has set its brand apart by connecting emotionally with customers. Think of a simple neighborhood bar where friends gather. Or a farmers market where growers and shoppers swap stories. Pepperdine University professor Mark Mallinger told *Fortune* magazine, "They [Trader Joe's] see themselves as a national chain of neighborhood specialty grocery stores. It means you want to create an image of mom and pop as you grow."[2] People love the atmosphere so much that it breaks down the barriers between strangers. If you want to make new friends, they are waiting for you at Trader Joe's.

It turns out that conversation is the way the store has empathized with customers since the beginning. Rather than relying on traditional market research, the company has fostered in each of its 365 stores a time-honored tradition of observing and listening. Employees are taught to anticipate people's unstated needs by watching to see if they can add a bit of helpful information during a customer's visit. Highly personalized service is what you get at Trader Joe's, with a large splash of creativity just to make you feel good. All the in-store artwork is handmade by staff artists. Brightly colored murals and chalkboards are everywhere to brighten the day—and intrigue the customers.

I spoke to Mike, a "crew member" in West Hollywood. He was decked out in the Hawaiian shirt that many staffers wear to convey the idea of a casual, tropical island. "We love our customers," Mike said. "Especially the eccentric ones. They keep us on our toes when it comes to listening. Their ideas can get a little out there, but that's all part of the experience here. Were all a little crazy, aren't we?" Mike explained that hiring the right kind of employee makes all the difference for the company. The company's job application says: "The most important role for the Crew is to deliver a great customer experience. The Crew creates a fun, warm and friendly shopping experience throughout the store. They share their product knowledge and enthusiasm with customers by answering questions, offering suggestions, and walking customers to products. The Crew makes sure our customers know they are welcome and cared for."

New hires are trained in what's called "Customer Experience: A Trader Joe's Love Story." They are expected to "love" their customers by proactively greeting them; making meaningful eye contact, and helping them find whatever their heart desires. Within limits, of course.

In his book *Paradox of Choice*, psychologist Barry Schwartz explained that customers often feel confused and bewildered when given too many choices. Upon a visit to his local supermarket he counted 285 types of cookies, ninety-five snack choices, twenty-two types of frozen waffles, and eight different pain relievers.[3] This large number of choices, fueled by brand extensions and endless variations, has been the typical retailer's path toward a kind of mass customization. It's become a way of saying we have something for everyone. Yet the dizzying array of choices often results in less purchasing. Recent studies have proven time and again that people become paralyzed when faced with too much stuff.[4]

Trader Joe's solves this by paring down store offerings to between two thousand and four thousand products per store. The typical grocery store stocks more than fifty thousand items.[5] But Trader Joe's isn't content to just keep selling the same old things. It has a reputation for product innovation, often driven by ideas generated by—you guessed it—their customers. The constantly evolving product mix makes every trip to Trader Joe's like an adventure in foodie paradise. And it works well: Trader Joe's produces $1,300 per square foot in sales.[6] That's at least double the industry average.

One of the secrets to Trader Joe's ability to profit from the Power of the Heart is that it has really turned every local store into a community innovation laboratory. While passionate and loyal customers are engaged in active shopping, they are also actively discussing what they're doing with store employees who are trained to be highly attentive. Because managers (called Captains and Mates) spend the majority of their days on the floor, they look for every possible opportunity to interact with customers. If a customer is not sure she will like something, an employee is happy to rip open a bag or a box to let her try it with no obligation to buy. When is the last time you shopped in any kind of store where the staff was willing to open the products for you to test?

TJ's doesn't need focus groups because its employees are actively involved in the daily lives of their customers. One Trader Joe's executive put it this way: "We feel really close to our customers. When we want to know what's on their minds, we don't need to put them in a sterile room with a swinging bulb."[7] Trader

Joe's has figured out the Power of the Heart. The more they know their customers, the more they love them. And obviously, the feeling is mutual.

The Bank with a Difference

I hate my bank. You can't trust them because they are from Wall Street. They could care less about my problems or me. But, what's the point of changing? They are all the same and you have to bank somewhere.

Wanda, Kansas City, Missouri
Participant in a focus group about retail banking

On a cold December evening I listened carefully to Wanda and nineteen other bank customers in Kansas City discuss their attitudes about the state of the banking industry. Little did Wanda know that five thousand miles away, a company had already heard her complaints and was doing something to permanently alter the relationship between a banking institution and its customers by understanding the Power of the Heart.

There have been three generations of banks. The first was the fortress bank, simply a safe place to keep your money. Service was sparse because there was minimal competition. Banks could set all the rules. They could keep their own hours, closing at three o'clock in the afternoon, for example. It mattered little if the customer was inconvenienced; the bank's job was to protect the money, not try to grow it.

The second generation was the reluctant marketer bank. In the 1980s, banking was deregulated in an effort to spur competition, and it worked. At first, bankers didn't know how to compete except to offer a free premium, like a toaster, if you opened a checking account. But as competition increased, the level of market segmentation and sophistication did as well.

Today, the third generation is the differentiator bank. We have witnessed so much consolidation that it is hard to know the players without a program. But in Denmark there's a bank that is paying huge dividends. In this case, three unlikely entities merged, entities you wouldn't normally combine: a bank, a butik, and a bibliotek (bank, store, and library).

Jyske (pronounced Yeeska) Bank is headquartered in Silkeborg, Denmark. With a population of only forty-three thousand, the city is less than a tenth of the size of Kansas City. But the Customer CEO changes introduced by Jyske over the past decade have introduced a revolution of choice in the conservative banking industry. Jyske Bank has been intensely studied and its innovative ideas are rippling across the globe. Jyske realized that it had an opportunity to reinvent itself, even though the business was doing well. But executives felt the bigger risk was to rest on their laurels and do nothing.

To set themselves apart, the bank created Jyske Differences, which focused on four areas: people, facilities, marketing, and customer counseling tools. The bank collaborated with the Copenhagen Institute for Future Studies, a social science think tank, to explore emerging trends for customers.[8] Jyske teams spent time in the field studying Starbucks and Apple Stores, and observed that they were making deep, emotional connections to their customers. This was unlike anything banks had ever done. Customers also felt that personal financial decisions were hard because the product choices were often too abstract. People needed more concrete and tangible ways to understand the wide array of bank products and services. Customer interviews found that, to most people, banks were cold, detached places that did little to understand the needs of their customers.

The bank wrote a manifesto called *Our Foundations* to publicly outline what Jyske really stood for.[9] This document sent a clear message both internally and externally that this bank was really different. Here's just a brief portion.

> Our core values are carved in stone. They are common to us all and govern the way we behave towards each other. In

the eyes of both customers and employees, our values are what make us special.

Our values are:

- Common sense
- Being open and honest
- Being different and unpretentious
- Showing genuine interest and equal respect
- Being efficient and persevering

To get it right, Jyske knew that the bank and its employees had to sincerely "demonstrate insight and respect for other people." Employees were trained to provide the customer with an "experience" like none other. This meant supporting their customers and helping them fulfill their dreams. Some customers were recent university graduates beginning new careers. Others needed help maximizing savings as they built their families. Some were working toward a more secure retirement. The bank switched to using a team concept, with specialists trained to help solve specific financial problems and provide advice for every need.

Jyske started calling each branch a "shop." Upon entering a shop, you see a wide-open, well-lit store that pulls you inside. You are greeted by a concierge who directs you to the area you need. At the entry you also see a large, ugly catfish, a whimsical icon for Jyske since 1982. Instead of a teller's window, you find a Money-Bar for quick bank services. The Market Square features banking products packaged in boxes, similar to the way software is displayed at computer stores. The boxes can be scanned—when they are, a video pops up on a flat screen and explains features and benefits. Every shop features an "Oasis," which looks like a library and has current magazines and books about personal finance. And of course there is the Jyske CoffeeBar. The bank wants to have the world's best coffee. Jyske customers loved this mix of places. Shops became special community gathering places.[10]

The bank's success with these changes has been remarkable. Deposits and customers soared over the past decade because Jyske successfully tapped into the Power of the Heart by engaging customers with empathy. It has created a culture and a place that truly cater to what its customers need.

We've now seen how some old-line businesses like grocery and banking transformed themselves through emotional connection. What about the same kind of results when it comes to rethinking sweaty workout clothes?

Can You Feel the Love?

Gravity is not on our side as we age, you know? I love LuLu because they understand that I want to look fit. I'm willing to pay a little more because they get it right.

Sherry, Atlanta, Georgia
Participant in a focus group about workout apparel

When I entered a Lululemon store for the first time, it immediately brought to mind that famous 1966 Beach Boys song "Good Vibrations," with its line about "the colorful clothes she wears." It's a brand that sells a rainbow of workout clothing for yoga, Pilates, and running enthusiasts. Or for women who just want to look good, like Sherry from the Atlanta focus group.

It seems that some women are willing to pay nearly $100 for workout pants that they claim feel better, last longer, and make their posteriors look like a million bucks.

Lululemon Athletica sells more than $1 billion worth of colorful clothes in a $14 billion a year market.[11] With fewer than 120 stores, the company produces the fourth highest sales per square foot in North America, behind only Apple, Tiffany, and Coach stores. Founder Chip Wilson is known as a kind of new-age capitalist guru, preaching positive thinking and prosperity for all. He says he wants to make the world a better place through transformational and motivational thinking. Wilson says, "I can't imagine what else I would do. This is the most difference I can make in the world."[12]

"I've been shopping at LuLu for about a year now," said Susan, another participant in our Atlanta focus group. "What strikes me is that they really listen intently to their customers. There's a chalkboard where people write their ideas about how to improve the products. They are constantly asking what I think. That's a lot different than anywhere else I have ever shopped."

Lululemon visually embraces the Power of the Heart. Every store displays dozens of short, bold messages of inspiration like "Love," "Do one thing a day that scares you," and "Friends are more important than money." The messages also feature more practical life tips, like "Do not use cleaning chemicals on your kitchen counter or floors. Someone will inevitably make a sandwich on your counter." The store also emblazons these thoughts on its shopping bags so everyone can "Feel the love."

The company doesn't believe in using focus groups or traditional market research, believing that the greatest insights lie within the four walls of its stores. According to the *Wall Street Journal*, Lululemon doesn't rely on big data generated through its website either. "Big data gives you a false sense of security," says CEO Christine Day. She prefers a hands-on approach, hanging out in her stores to take the measure of what her customers really say.[13]

It's clear that the company takes its approach to research very seriously. It willingly acknowledges that customer understanding is the "secret sauce" to innovation going forward. Day and her staff scour each store's weekly information to fine-tune every detail of the company's products and service. That's important, because the brand has new and growing competition from brands like Athleta, a division of The Gap. Athleta employs a strategy of siting stores near Lululemon locations and underpricing them by 10 to 15 percent. Lululemon loyalists like Susan don't seem the least bit interested. "I am loyal to LuLu. I'm not going to desert them just to save a few bucks," she said.

Lululemon also believes it has a not-so-secret research force. Before opening a location, the company aggressively recruits certified yoga, Pilates, dance, and fitness instructors in the local community. In exchange for 15 percent discounts, Lululemon seeks constant feedback on its products' design, fit, and quality. The company wants to expose its products to constant scrutiny and field-testing by real athletes and trainers.

The real trick to Lululemon's emotional connection with customers is based on the idea that a woman who feels better about how she looks will become a raving enthusiast. Our friend Sherry in Atlanta summed up this notion when she said, "My butt looks good." It looks like Lululemon has found a unique formula to put the Customer CEO in charge. By tapping into the Power of the Heart (and other physical attributes) it has created good vibrations for customers, employees, and stakeholders.

Profiting from the Power of the Heart

If you use empathy to gain a deeper, emotional connection with your customers, your business will thrive through passion. Passion ignites every aspect of a business's performance. When we look at Trader Joe's, Jyske Bank, and Lululemon, we see examples of three different ways to transform your enterprise.

As competition in every industry intensifies, strategy execution isn't enough. You have to cut through the competitive battlefield by touching hearts. Customers desire to do business with companies that are willing to connect and make them feel better. Simply put, your job is to move them from pain to gain. Every experience with your brand needs to resonate deeply within them. This can only happen if you are willing to understand your customers emotionally. Every great salesperson knows that most people buy based on emotional fulfillment rather than on a rational set of features or facts. Do you really know what your best prospects feel? What they fear? What frustrates them the most? Do you know what they dream about? Can you find meaningful ways to connect with them to help them achieve those dreams? Here are some key takeaways.

People Are Emotional

We all want—and need—to connect. Modern life seems to have washed away a sense of community. But people were meant to be social creatures. While digital social media is growing, it can't replace a smile, a friendly word, and an attitude that says, "I want to help you." Your environments, whether they are stores, call centers, or websites, have to offer ways for this connection to thrive. Jyske Bank transformed old-school banking products into new ways to help people realize their dreams. That's emotional. Lululemon sells expensive workout wear to women by selling them on an emotional appeal that they will look slimmer. Trader Joe's creates emotional experiences by talking and listening. Who could imagine that being listed as a competitive advantage in a corporate strategic planning document? But it is.

People Want to Smile

The world can be a downer and life is often pretty grim. There is a natural desire to escape to a better place. History shows us that, particularly during tough economic times, people need to get away from the troubles that weigh them down. Trader Joe's gives people a place to come that is like an oasis, where people talk to each other. Jyske literally created an Oasis in every shop. And the more your people connect through humor and happiness, the more they are energized and transformed themselves. What's not to like about happier customers and employees?

People Want to Love Your Stuff

Whatever you make or sell, customers want to do more than just tolerate it or like it; they want to love it! Are you creating products, services, and experiences that are up to the challenge? No one is going to embrace you if you are trying to peddle yesterday's news. It's out of date and out of sync with what people are looking for. Chip Wilson recognized that the only alternative for active women was ugly, poor-fitting workout clothing, so he created a look they could love. Trader Joe's gets people actively involved in using all of their senses to love both the food and the experiences they will find at the store.

Just as important as voice of the customer must be heart of the customer. Create innovative ways for customers to express themselves. Acknowledge their feelings. Each of the companies explored in this chapter has introduced interesting methods for customers to give real feedback. Don't be afraid of being a little less rational and a whole lot more passionate. The truth is, you cannot help but become more passionate when you let the Customer CEO love you. Bottom line: It's a lot tougher for your competitors to imitate love and passion.

(How well does your organization engage the Power of the Heart? Visit customerceopowercheck.com to download our free diagnostic tool.)

7

The Power of Simple

Key Customer CEO Question:

Why is this so complicated?

Chauncey Gardiner spoke with quiet confidence when he said, "In the garden, growth has its seasons. First comes spring and summer, but then we have fall and winter. And then we get spring and summer again."

Gardiner was a character brilliantly played by Peter Sellers in the 1979 movie, *Being There*. He was a simple man suddenly thrust into a complicated world. In a Hollywood twist, he accidently becomes an advisor to the rich and powerful, including the president of the United States. What was hailed as a commonsense metaphor about coming economic prosperity was really nothing more than mindless drivel spouted by a man who was a mere gardener. His name was actually Chance. Chance the gardener.

Being There was entertaining and a great piece of satire. But the deeper truth is that we all seek simplicity in a world seemingly gone mad with complexity. I have a poster on my office wall with a quote by musician and civil rights advocate Charles Mingus, who once said, "Making the simple complicated is commonplace; making the complicated simple, that's creativity."[1]

In my customer research work over the years, I have heard this sentiment expressed hundreds of times about every kind of product and service. The key Customer CEO question "Why is this so complicated?" comes from years of hearing frustrated customers who don't understand how companies could screw things up so badly. I remember a focus group I did in Houston, Texas, for an office equipment manufacturer. None of the office managers we were interviewing could understand why a leading global brand had decided to create such a complicated machine. It featured a dizzying array of options, switches, and glowing lights. The consensus of the group was that the product was a giant disaster because all they really needed was a "big red button" to turn it on and off. The company should have taken the time to listen before it designed the machine. But, as so often happens, the company thought it knew better. The engineers loaded up the product with complexity because, pure and simple, they could. The machine was withdrawn in less than a year due to underwhelming market response.

The good news is that a trickle of simplicity may be turning into a raging river. There is finally a *revolution of simplification* taking shape in the marketplace. When we look at technology innovations like the cloud, software as a service, analytics dashboards, and apps we see that developers are finally beginning to think about simplicity as a major driver of new business opportunities.

Great designers and inventors focus on reducing unnecessary steps. Take the simple metal zippers in our clothing. A zipper will eventually get stuck, lose teeth, and break. It took Swiss inventor

George de Mestral's random act of removing burrs from his dog's fur to imagine the possibilities that became his invention, Velcro. He noticed that the burrs were actually made up of tiny hooks.[2] Larry Miller invented the elliptical trainer after observing his daughter run.[3] In *Pursuit of Elegance*, author Matthew May explains why simplicity is such an important goal: "Because by nature we tend to add when we should subtract, and act when we should stop and think. Because we need some way to consistently replace value-destroying complexity with value-creating simplicity. Because we need to know how to make room for more of what matters by eliminating what doesn't."[4]

Customers are tired of so many choices everywhere they look. Remember the dilemma outlined by psychologist Barry Schwartz regarding excessive grocery store product choices? It becomes overwhelming. When there are too many choices, the brain shuts down and defaults to the familiar brands it knows and loves. No one has the time and energy to figure it all out. In a Harvard Business Review blog post, it was reported that a corporate executive board's survey of seven thousand consumers worldwide found customers are "overwhelmed by the volume of choice and information they're exposed to, and marketers' relentless efforts to 'engage' with them."[5]

I believe every business should strive to become a simple business. Every product, service, and experience you ask customers to acquire should be simple to buy, use, maintain, and get rid of when it's used up or worn out. The more people can enjoy something because of its simplicity, the more often they will use and recommend it to others.

Let's take a look at four Customer CEO companies that succeed at simple.

Number Two and Lovin' It

Last week, I thought I would try a California Bacon Club. They had a big picture of one on their menu board but the guy behind the counter didn't even know what it was. He had to go ask his manager. I just wanted to eat and get out of there while they stood around debating it. I needed to get back to work. Why offer it if you don't even know what it is?

Francisco, Miami, Florida
Participant in a focus group about fast food restaurants

In March of 2000, my friend, filmmaker and director Ed Schumacher, picked me up at Los Angeles International Airport (LAX), and we headed for lunch. In less than five minutes he pulled up to a small restaurant on South Sepulveda Boulevard. The restaurant was sitting almost directly across the Pacific Coast Highway from LAX runway 24R. There was a line of people waiting to get inside. This was my introductory visit to an American cultural phenomenon known simply as In-N-Out Burger. As we entered the restaurant, Ed assured me I was in for a special meal. He explained that, since moving to LA from Florida ten years earlier, hardly a week had gone by that he hadn't made an In-N-Out visit because it wasn't just a typical fast food hamburger joint. It turns out he was right.

In-N-Out Burger isn't the kind of place that would offer anything as exotic as a California Bacon Club. With more than 230 stores in only a handful of states, it has quietly become the number-two hamburger restaurant in America based upon sales per store. At nearly $2 million per unit, In-N-Out Burger runs second only to McDonalds.[6] And since 1948, it has continued to thrive through the Power of Simple. In an industry that usually features complicated menus that cause customers to waste time by standing and staring while trying to figure out what to order, In-N-Out is straightforward, with just five basic items. The company has never tried to be all things to all people. Late founder Harry Snyder summed up In-N-Out Burger's simple mission by saying, "Keep it real simple, do one thing and do it the best you can."[7]

For more than a half century, since 1948, In-N-Out has

amazingly stayed the course: sell fresh, great-tasting hamburgers, French fries, and milk shakes. It has avoided the temptation to offer breakfast, kids' meals, salads, pizza, chicken, fish, or exotic sandwich variations. By sticking to its core business, it delivers a cost structure much better than that of McDonalds or any other chain. The company doesn't waste valuable floor space, inventory, and maintenance costs supporting marginal products. It has built a competitive advantage by leaving those low-volume items to its competitors.

In her book *In-N-Out Burger: A Behind the Counter Look at the Fast-Food Chain That Breaks All the Rules*, author Stacy Perman explored the phenomenon of the restaurant that Harry built:

> The little regional chain that was built on a philosophy of quality, made-to-order hamburgers, and "the customer is always king" had over the years drawn fans from every imaginable quarter. In an industry that has come to be seen as a scourge on modern society, responsible for everything from obesity to urban blight to cultural imperialism, this modest, low-slung eatery with the big yellow arrow is unique among fast-food breeds: a chain revered by hamburger aficionados and epicureans, anti-globalization fanatics and corporate raiders, meat-eaters and even vegetarians. Make mention of the three monosyllabic words and a kind of reverie takes hold. People's eyes close and their lips begin to quiver with the pleasures of sense memory.[8]

In-N-Out Burger illustrates how you can beat your competitors by being a Customer CEO company. Rather than falling in love with the idea of being innovative in terms of product development, it has succeeded by becoming master of the basics in a commoditized business. It is the best at *simply* delivering on the core product that customers crave. By keeping things simple, the company reduces mistakes and shortens learning curves. In-N-Out defies conventional wisdom in the fast food industry: there are no freezers, microwaves, or hot racks to keep food warm or to heat things back up. Everything is fresh and made to order. Paradoxically, In-N-Out Burger has become one of the most innovative companies in America by not being innovative.

From the beginning, what customers thought about every detail of the restaurant was critically important to the company. This desire to listen closely was born of humility and an obligation to provide the best experience possible. Harry Snyder's goal was to always serve both customers and employees. The late Rich Snyder, who succeeded his father as CEO in the early 1990s and served until he was killed in a plane crash, believed in the idea illustrated with the Upside-Down Org Chart in chapter 1. Snyder used an inverted pyramid as a symbol instead. He practiced servant-based leadership and saw his job as CEO at the bottom of the pyramid, not the top.

According to Perman, Synder believed, "He was there to support everyone else in the company. When talking to store managers, he was always careful to refer to the shops as 'your stores' and never asked them 'What store do you manage?' He wanted them to have pride of ownership. Regardless of anyone's position or length of time with the company, Rich treated everyone equally and as if they were all special."[9]

The Snyders had always shown their people they cared by the way they paid employees. From the outset, employees at every level were paid better than their counterparts at the competition. The Snyders recognized that loyal, happy employees would have contagious enthusiasm and that customers would respond. The result was one of the lowest turnover rates in the volatile fast food industry. "They have the lowest turnover rate in the fast food industry, which is notorious for turnover," says Perman. "They say that the average manager's tenure is 14 years, but they have managers who have been there 30 or 40 years."[10]

In-N-Out's dedication to the Power of Simple should be contagious for every business. Focus on producing a quality product, treat people well, be consistent, and success will follow. Think about this for a minute and consider how it applies to your enterprise. How has In-N-Out outlasted and prospered while literally thousands of other eating establishments failed over the decades? I believe that we tend to get too caught up in complex strategic planning rather than simple execution. We constantly worry about getting knocked off by established or upstart competitors so we attempt to shield ourselves from every potential risk. Unfortunately, this diverts our attention from just *simply* getting the job done for our customers. As we see with In-N-Out, customers will richly reward you for creating simple.

Why Didn't I Think of That?

I love Zinfandel. But I don't drink it very often because opening the bottle is a real hassle and it spoils before I can finish it.
Sarah, Chicago, Illinois
Participant in a customer interview about wine

Benjamin Franklin once said that wine is "a constant proof that God loves us, and loves to see us happy." For American fans of wines from Napa Valley and Sonoma, nothing could be truer. The worth of California wines became recognized around the world in 1976 at an event called the Judgment of Paris. Two relatively unknown California wines, the 1973 Chateau Montelena Chardonnay and the 1973 Stag's Leap Wine Cellars Cabernet Sauvignon from Napa competed in a blind test against better-known French wines. And both Napa wines won.[11] This was a monumental moment in wine history, and it set the stage for thirty years of explosive growth in the American wine industry. There was also a popular movie made about the Judgment, called *Bottle Shock*, based loosely on what happened at the event. The French winemaking industry had enjoyed a virtual monopoly on what was considered great wine until the emergence of this new breed of winemaker.

The wine world has changed much since 1976, with global

imports of every variety. It truly is a global village of wine. Australian winery Casella Wines reinvented the category in the early 2000s with its Yellow Tail brand. The winery developed a product that focused on winning the nontraditional wine-drinking market by capturing people who prefer beer and cocktails. Casella found that an entirely new market could be captured if it offered a simpler, sweeter product that didn't require a high level of wine sophistication to enjoy.[12]

In fact, Yellow Tail tackled wine snobbery by figuring out that many customers were intimidated by the terms and complexity often associated with wine drinking. Debate rages on in the wine world about fruitiness, tannins, and aging, but what about the bottle the wine is sold in? Was there a way to make the packaging of wine more accessible to people like Sarah? In other words, was there a simpler way to drink wine?

The best ideas usually create those "Why didn't I think of that?" moments in us. Meet Vinoware, an idea that answers so many customer issues it is shocking no one has done it before. It's a radical new kind of wine container that's part stemless wine glass and part corkless bottle. A California company called Stacked Wines has jumped into the middle of the Power of Simple. The product stacks four individually sealed containers made of lightweight, high-quality, shatterproof, recyclable plastic. Each "cup" is sealed with a top like you would find on a yogurt container.

Three University of California, Irvine, students developed the idea and won "Best Concept Paper," but they kept going until they turned their Stacked Wine into a real product. "The concept of individual wine glasses seems so obvious. We're all amazed no one has thought of it before, but it seems that's how a lot of great ideas are born. I'm hopeful that Stacked Wines will become as commonplace as individual servings of other beverages," said Jodi Wynn, the company's cofounder and vice president of marketing and business operations.[13]

Writer Conor Friedersdorf summed up the need for easier-opening wine bottles: "Being a forgetful sort, I've had occasion to force corks down the necks of bottles with objects as varied as a cheap plastic pen, splintery driftwood, a friend's lipstick container, and the curved metal protruding from a u-lock."[14]

The new brand solves many obvious problems for wine drinkers. If you want to go mobile for a picnic, hike, or camping trip, it works. Customers can peel, pour, and drink without bringing a corkscrew and glasses. And because the glasses are plastic, there's nothing to break. Stacked Wines also eliminates the problems of opening a full bottle that might not get drunk. A person can drink a cup at a time.

An unintended benefit of Stacked Wines was highlighted by the popular television host and author Dr. Mehmet Oz. He is a proponent of the health benefits of drinking a glass of red wine but complains that it is hard to accurately measure a glass. He extolled to his large national audience the virtue of the individual Stacked Wine cup, which holds approximately six ounces, a serving that equals only 140 calories.[15]

Of course, packaging will only get you so far. Stacked Wines won't last long unless the wine is well received by the market. So we decided to organize a blind wine tasting in Los Angeles. We wanted to see how people liked the wine when it was pitted against other well-known but unidentified wines. Five people were served three chardonnays and three merlots each. Two of our panelists preferred the Stacked Wines chardonnay; the other three ranked it third. The Stacked merlot ranked first for three of our testers, while the other two ranked it second. Overall, it was a good night for Stacked Wines. Here are some of the comments people made after we revealed the brands they had tasted.

Lynne said, "The Chardonnay was really delicious. I could taste apple right away. But it didn't overpower me. I would buy this. I love the little cups." Scott told us, "The packaging is cool. Not the best merlot but good enough for a weekend to the mountains." Frank agreed. "I've had better, but it was really pretty nice and tasty. But, I think these guys will do well because they have made it so convenient to use." Brenda said, "I could taste the berries. It was really great! I will definitely be buying Stacked Wines." Paul was the one most sold on the wine: "They've done a fantastic job for a new brand. High quality, plus it's so simple. Really, really nice."

So far, so good, but the big payoff for Vinoware is that it has designed something so simple that it can easily replace current traditional products in the distribution system. A Stacked Wine package takes up the same shelf space as a traditional wine bottle at a reduced weight. The company sees a growing market because its wine is simply more accessible and easier to consume. That's the Power of Simple in action.

Sole Simplicity

I love shoes. What's it to you?

Veronica, San Antonio, Texas
Participant in a focus group about women's shoes

Carrie Bradshaw, played by actress Sarah Jessica Parker, was the famous narrator of HBO's *Sex and the City*. Often described as fashion-obsessed, Carrie was a shoe lover who particularly desired expensive shoes by high-end designers. And the more expensive the shoes, the better. According to her friend Miranda, played by Cynthia Nixon, Carrie was at least $40,000 poorer because of her love affair with shoes.[16] From Carrie's point of view, shoes, not diamonds, were a girl's best friend.

Dominique McClain Barteet is a real-life shoe aficionado. After years of international travel, she tired of packing and hauling multiple pairs of shoes from home to hotels and back again. When she found a pair in a style she liked, she would buy the shoes in several colors. Being a bit more practical than Carrie Bradshaw, she decided none of this made any sense. She wondered why no one had ever come up with a simpler shoe solution.

Why not have one base sole with interchangeable tops? That

way, a woman could customize the look of a shoe for any occasion, business, casual, or formal. This customized shoe could match any outfit. The key was being able to change it fast. Upon further investigation, she found that no manufacturer had yet thought of this idea, and she saw a ripe business opportunity because she knew that many women faced the same dilemma. According to Hoovers, a business research company, the U.S. shoe store industry has a combined annual revenue of about $27 billion.[17] Industry research publisher IBISWorld reports, "Women in the U.S. are more likely to purchases multiple pairs of shoes than women from most other parts of the world. Women's shoes regularly change in style, which allows for high competition levels between firms."[18]

Branding her shoe enterprise One Sole: The Original Interchangeable Shoe, Barteet first designed a comfortable and fashionable shoe. She was awarded multiple patents on her unique design, which features a set of snaps that secure the custom tops in place. As she began to show her idea to others, demand grew organically as small local stores wanted to carry the line. Customers started suggesting new designs, colors, and fabrics for the tops. In 2012, Barteet was asked to appear on the ABC network program *Shark Tank*.[19] For that reality show, entrepreneurs seeking funding appear before a panel of investors pitching their ideas. When Barteet appeared, she stunned the panel by announcing that she had sold nearly $20 million of shoes part time, while continuing to work as a pharmacist.

I convened a small group of three self-professed shoe-aholics in San Antonio, Texas, to understand why Barteet had hit the mark. Only one of the three women was familiar with One Sole, as she had seen Barteet's *Shark Tank* appearance. After showing them a pair of One Soles, it was clear why the product worked. It was simple.

Barbara said, "This is fantastic. I've been known to pack an extra bag just for my shoes. My husband will be very happy!" Jennifer saw the obvious benefit of saving money. "This is brilliant. As much as I love buying shoes, this will save me hundreds of dollars a year." When I showed them the One Sole website, which showcases literally thousands of tops, they were astounded at the sheer simplicity of the product. Veronica asked, "Why didn't anyone think of this before? This is one smart woman."

Barteet's One Sole shows what you can accomplish when you are willing to solve a problem that is right in front of you. Often, you only need to step back and see it. Barteet may have seen it herself in the beginning, but she immediately engaged with potential customers by asking them their ideas about how to build the line with new designs.

That's the Power of Simple.

Profiting from the Power of Simple

Complexity kills profitability. Simplicity is always a better choice. The truth is that no matter how good you think you are today, others are waiting to take you down. They will see a better way that will disrupt you. Upstarts will take advantage of your dependence on the status quo. You will profit over the long haul if you continue to focus on simplification. Every market will have someone who is the clear leader in simplicity.

Simplicity is what the Customer CEO is demanding and will find. Instead of offering a constantly changing menu, In-N-Out Burger has defied fast food logic by turning out a consistently great product. Stacked Wines saw what industry giants have always missed: a simpler way to serve wine for people who just want to enjoy a single glass or who want to take it along easily. One Sole enabled women to lighten their load and have a wider choice of shoe designs than ever before for a fraction of the price. Simple works. Here are some simple ideas about being simple.

Simplicity Requires Careful Observation

Observation is the way to stay engaged with your existing and potential customers going forward. Spend plenty of time in the field actively watching how customers are using products and services and experiencing brands. Find the pain points and simplify them as soon as possible. For example, One Sole allowed women to take along a lot of shoes by figuring out a new way to pack them and change them efficiently.

Don't Make the Customer Do Extra Work

If you make your customer do extra work, some upstart will come after you. I cannot emphasize this enough. People want to do *less* work. So figure out ways to do that undesirable work for them. Do not assume you are the only one thinking about this issue. You aren't. Look to reduce the amount of work a customer must do while using your product. By reducing the extra work involved in opening a bottle of wine, Stacked Wines found an entirely new market segment. Ask yourself, can my product or service be made any simpler?

Ask the Right Questions

When approaching the idea of simplicity, it's easy to ask the wrong questions. The right questions to ask up front about your product are:

- Do you believe there might be a better way to do this job? Why or why not?
- What if there was a product that could do the job much better? Would you buy it?

Whatever business you are in, start with the right questions. Once you learn whether you are onto something, get out into the field to observe people doing the job you are trying to make easier.

Reduce Complexity with Fewer Choices

Kill features and services that don't get used, and optimize the ones that do. Think about In-N-Out's menu board versus those at other quick-service restaurants. You don't have to offer something for everybody. Make a few really great things. Why clutter your choices?

Think End to End

Simplicity relates to the entire customer experience, from pricing to customer support. It's important to apply this thinking to every customer touch point as well. For example, when was the last time you sat down and had some customers try to navigate your website? If you haven't done this, you might be surprised at the disconnect between what they are trying to accomplish and the experience they are actually having.

Remember that the more complicated your products are, the fewer the people who can or will use them. No single Customer CEO power will open up the pipeline to new customers more than simplicity.

(How well does your organization engage the Power of Simple? Visit customerceopowercheck.com to download our free diagnostic tool.)

8

The Power of Yes

Key Customer CEO Question:

Why is your answer always no?

I grew up in the 1960s in Dallas, Texas, and I vividly remember a breezy little radio jingle that happily sang, "First National Bank says 'Yes'!" Even then, a long time before banks could spell the word "marketing," that locally owned downtown bank—or its ad agency—had figured out that customers were much more inclined to do business with you if you made doing business easy. The Power of Yes means, "We are here to serve you."

In his book *Quest for the Best*, the late Neiman Marcus chairman Stanley Marcus wrote, "Customers have the perception that service is an indication of interest in them as individuals, not just as robots dispensing money."[1] He said that going well beyond the call of duty would create "a state of euphoria, which in turn fosters loyalty."[2] If we claim to believe in customer service, doesn't that mean we believe in serving the customer more than serving ourselves—even if it means losing a sale today? What if a competitor offers a better solution to the problem the customer is seeking to solve? Will your frontline people recommend a competitor as a better solution in order to better serve the customer?

Many believe that the best Christmas movie of all time was *Miracle on 34th Street*.[3] In the story, the Macy's department store's kindly old Santa, played by actor Edmund Gwenn, would send mothers across the street to the dreaded competitor, Gimbels, to buy items Macy's didn't stock or if Gimbels offered a lower price.[4] Gimbels quickly adopted the same policy so it wouldn't look like a store run by greedy Scrooges at Christmastime. Finally, Mr. Macy and Mr. Gimbel shook hands and became allies, at least for that particular season. In the movie, they said yes. Why is it so hard to say yes in real life?

Jan Carlzon, former CEO of Scandinavian Airlines, told a story about the Mandarin Oriental Hotel Group in Asia.[5] He explained that the hotel's official policy was to not permit its frontline staff to say *no* to guests. The staff had to ask special permission from upper management to say no, and could do so only if they believed the guest's request was too extravagant. Carlzon became widely known and respected for what he called "moments of truth," and he titled his book *Moments of Truth: New Strategies for Today's Customer-Driven Economy.* He proposed that every contact with the customer is a moment of truth. In order to identify and create better moments of truth, companies have to shift from inside thinking to outside thinking. This becomes a "moment of magic." Customers expect and demand no less. This is the Power of Yes.

A few years ago, my wife bought me an expensive dress shirt for my birthday. Before wearing it, I dropped it at the neighborhood dry cleaners we had used for many years. I picked it up a few days later and noticed that the sleeves were torn and tattered, as if they had been run through some kind of paper shredder. I took it back and the manager blamed it on the material the shirt was made of, telling me it wasn't really their fault. I was stunned, and reminded her that we had spent more money than I could remember at her store for more than a decade. They were our exclusive cleaners and had gotten 100 percent of our business. We were the very definition of loyal customers. I explained that the shirt had cost over $100 and had never been worn. But it didn't faze her a bit. She said, "We'll give you a $25 credit for your next order but we're not going to replace the shirt." I never returned. She only had the power to say no, and it cost her company thousands of dollars in lost revenue from me and from everyone I told about the incident. That cleaners flunked its moment of truth by practicing the power of no.

In researching this book, I was tempted to write about Customer CEO companies that masterfully understand the Power of Yes, like Nordstrom and Ritz-Carlton Hotels. Those are exceptional companies that truly love their customers. But I wanted to focus on some lesser-known examples to serve as inspirations for businesses of all sizes. If you look carefully, you can see "yes" in some unexpected places. Let's take a look at the Power of Yes.

The World Is Flat

At a time when "customer service" seems to be a dying art, I was kind of surprised to find it in spades in a tire store—and a discount chain tire store at that. I had an error in my TPMS (tire pressure monitoring system) that my mechanic could only half diagnose. He had the tool to read the computer error code and find out that the transmitter in one of the tires was no longer transmitting a signal. Unfortunately, he did not have the tool to determine WHICH transmitter was dead. I called the cursed dealership (I hate you with a white-hot passion) and was told I'd have to leave my car overnight for them to diagnose the problem, they'd charge me a diagnostic fee of $99.50, and they refused *to give me even a rough estimate of how much it would cost to replace the sensor until after THEY diagnosed the problem.*

My mechanic recommended that I call Discount Tire instead. They said to come on by, they had the correct diagnostic tool and they'd happily diagnose the problem for free. And why wouldn't they? I watched the process, which took exactly 2 minutes and involved holding a receiver next to each tire to see if the transmitter was sending a signal. Good on Discount Tire. Another boo (but not a surprising boo) for (the dealer) for finding yet another way to hose their customers. After confirming the problem, the guy at Discount Tire quoted me $75 for the part, which they unfortunately did not have on hand, and sent me on my way. A few hours later he called to let me know the part had arrived and scheduled a convenient time to have it installed. I arrived at my scheduled time and was immediately taken care of. A tech showed me the part and told me what he was going to do. He did the job, walked me through what he had done, and sent me on my way, all in under 15 minutes. In the 15 minutes I was in the shop, I watched clerks and technicians alike addressing customers and one another with respect. The techs looked like they enjoyed what they were doing, too.

Are any of you other businesses out there listening? THIS is how you get people to come back. THANK YOU, Discount Tire. You blew my mind today. I will be back for all tire and tire-related needs. I just wish I could send all my other service providers to you for training. If my doctor's office ran like Discount Tire, I'd actually make an appointment and go!

Robyn, Austin, Texas[6]
Reviewer of Discount Tire on yelp.com

Imagine building a $3 billion business by giving stuff away for free to complete strangers. That's what one company has done for the Robyns of the world. And for me, too.

Odds are you have never heard of Discount Tire. Although the company has eight hundred stores, they are located in only twenty-three states. It captures about a 10 percent share of the U.S. tire market. It's one of those businesses you only think about when you need it. Discount Tire is a quiet company that doesn't even belong to its industry trade association. "We like to let our actions speak louder than our words," CEO Tom Englert said.[7] Discount Tire may be quiet but its embrace of the Power of Yes speaks loudly. "Our store managers and employees are empowered to do whatever it takes to satisfy the customer," Englert said. "There is a great autonomy in our stores that helps them meet the individual needs of the customers in their particular areas."[8]

The company estimates that it says yes at least six thousand times a day to people who just want a flat tire fixed. Discount Tire fixes these flats for free. The company leaves a significant amount of money on the table today in order to generate up-front loyalty before the purchase. That's how I first became a customer. I can't remember the precise year I first heard of Discount Tire. I couldn't believe that a store would fix something for free if it hadn't originally sold me the product. But founder Bruce Halle explains that people are very grateful for having their tires repaired at no charge and "we've made a customer for life, probably."[9] In my case, that's exactly what happened. I have lost count of the number of tires I have purchased from the company over the years. My wife and I estimate that we have had at least thirty encounters with Discount Tire. We cannot recall any negative experiences, only positive ones. Employees don't try to up-sell you, they just answer your questions and get you back on the road as fast as possible.

Discount Tire's Power of Yes culture stems from Halle's ideas about treating customers and employees like family. He told industry publication *Tire Business* that from the beginning he wanted "to treat people fairly and to just be nice."[10] As a customer, I've been told by store employees that they didn't want me driving on unsafe tires. While that may seem like a small thing, it speaks volumes about the deeper connection the company feels for its customers.

Notice that Discount Tire has stayed the course by selling and servicing only tires and wheels. The shops don't change oil, do front-end alignments, or sell other add-ons. Michael Rosenbaum, author of *Six Tires, No Plan*, which chronicled the company's story, explains, "All of these issues would be of great importance if the company was selling tires, but the significance declines greatly when one realizes that the company's product isn't the tires, but the tire replacement experience."[11] Halle understood that no customer *wants* to buy new tires. It's a giant pain that takes you away from more important pursuits. Customers *need*, no, make that *have to*, buy new tires. This is an incredibly important distinction. This is where the Power of Yes lives. Halle turned an unpleasant situation into a positive experience that builds deep and abiding loyalty.

King of the Castles

The worst thing for me is that no matter what we tell a host hotel, they always seem to get it wrong. Planning a big event can take us a year but in those two or three days on-site I age ten years. No matter how much we spell things out or scream and yell, nothing ever seems to change.

Louise, New York City
Participant in a customer interview about corporate planning and hotels

Louise speaks for every event planner I have ever met. For the most part, planners are serious professionals, laser focused on pulling off their events to perfection. They say that the one thing they can be certain of is uncertainty. Whether the event is for six or six thousand attendees, planners know there will always be problems. In recent years, the situation has been magnified as hotels and other venues have reduced staff and become dependent on technology to take care of the minutia. Of course, this affects every participant.

Recently, I was speaking to a group of three hundred attendees at a national trade association at one of the largest hotels in Las Vegas. As usual, I checked in with the conference organizers early to test the room's setup for my presentation. When I plugged in my laptop there was zero sound for the video portion of the presentation. The room was nearly filled before the audio video guy showed up. I was sweating it because the video we had produced for the session was critical. The planner was distraught, and essentially threatened the guy with his life. Two minutes before showtime, we finally had sound. He smiled and said, "Break a leg." Just an everyday occurrence in the event planning business, no doubt.

The stress of all of this uncertainty wasn't good for Jacques Horovitz. He grew so frustrated with the poor level of service for conferences and events that he decided to do something completely different. He launched his own venue. He founded Châteauform' in 1996 with a single location in France. Now his business encompasses thirty-three locations in seven European countries. Horovitz explained:

> I have been organizing residential seminars for executive committees, management meetings, and every type of department across Europe, Asia, and the Americas for over 30 years. I have always been struck by how poorly venues cater for such events. Sometimes the meeting rooms are uncomfortable or badly equipped, sometimes the venues themselves are unsuitable—they are frequently too large and participants feel lost among other groups, wedding parties, business people, and holidaymakers.[12]

Imagine a place set up for businesspeople to actually take care of their business. And these are not nondescript locations in crowded urban centers: these are beautiful, expansive, old-world villas and castles. Châteauform' venues combine historic European architecture with modern technology so that customers can work, team build, dine, and relax. In the mood for a quiet planning meeting surrounded by antiques from the Italian Renaissance? Try the Villa Gallarati Scotti in Vimercate, Italy. Feel like holding a sales conference with a Swiss mountain experience? There's Le Chalet de Champéry, in a Swiss alpine village at the foot of the Portes du Soleil's four hundred miles of ski slopes. Perhaps you would like to hold a board meeting while sampling some British history at Châteauform' at Hever. It's part of the estate that was once childhood home to King Henry VIII's second wife, Anne Boleyn. Of course, there's no better place on earth to brainstorm than at a castle in the heart of the French Beaujolais wine country, La Maison des Contes, situated among the vines in the Rhône river valley.

As you can see, these are not your everyday meeting facilities. It's hard to imagine much work getting done there, isn't it? But this is the genius of Horovitz's concept. His team has created perfect places to say yes to a clientele that is usually told no by venues that treat them like cattle. The locations may seem extravagant, but they are considerably less expensive than urban choices. They are situated in small villages in the countryside, usually about an hour from a major airport. Châteauform' tells planners that its venues are not hotels with cut-and-paste meeting rooms but high-tech "elegant yet comfortable properties set in private parkland well away from the hubbub of city life, offering an environment conducive to strategic thinking, productive meetings, team-building, and relaxation."[13] Besides the beautiful surroundings of its locations, why is Châteauform' truly the "home of seminars"?

The key piece of the company's business model is an on-site husband-and-wife management team. These are highly experienced hospitality experts who deliver concierge service, one group at a time. They share in the profit of their facility, so they are incentivized to build long-term relationships with their customers by saying yes. They fulfill the needs of their most important customers, the event planners, by delivering remarkable events. Instead of wondering whether the food will be ready or the projectors will work, planners can relax. Each Châteauform' management couple is trained to continually adapt to each event's specific needs. If there's a special request or a last-minute change, the answer is always *yes*. Instead of corporate rigidity and rules, the company actively promotes its flexibility.

At the heart of the experience is the meeting room. The company understands how important atmospherics are to a successful outcome, including lighting, temperature, comfortable seating, and technology. Many rooms are outfitted with the latest technology, including interactive touch screens and smart boards. The facilities are very exclusive, designed to support only a small number of business groups meeting at the same time. Under no circumstances are there tourists like you would encounter in a typical hotel. Châteauform' also offers world-class food prepared by full-time chefs as well as plentiful recreational diversions designed to promote team building.

At Châteauform' they love to say, "Everything is possible, you just need to ask!" Customers are encouraged to suggest any out-of-the-box idea that will make their sessions better. The staff knows that the whole point of a few days away from the office for busy executive teams is both to conduct some important business and to improve their collaboration and productivity. The company also reviews customer feedback through what they call love or loathe letters.

Marion Debruyne, partner and associate professor of Vlerick Leuven Ghent Management School in Belgium, wrote about the importance of customer insight at Châteauform': "Being a customer-focused organization requires continuous listening to customer demands and feedback. At Châteauform' that means processing 5 million 'Sweet or Sour' customer satisfaction surveys a year. But it also means a culture of continuous adaptations in small and big changes to the offering to respond to customer concerns. Innovation and customer focus go hand in hand." Horovitz puts the Power of Yes into action because of his attitude toward his customers. Debruyne explains, "Profit is not the ultimate goal. Making happy customers is. And oops, what do you know, that tends to lead to profitability! Happy customers means spontaneous word-of-mouth, lower marketing costs, higher loyalty, increased share of wallet, lower price sensitivity…all driving profitable growth." Yes, profit happens when you allow the Power of Yes to live and grow within an enterprise.[14]

Let's Partner Up

I handle all the contract administration for five states. We usually have at least twenty projects going on all the time. Guys like me don't have the time to tell these equipment salesmen all about our business every time they drop in. If they want our business, they need to know something about us before they show up. And don't act like a know-it-all.

Norman, Ft. Worth, Texas
Participant in a focus group about business-to-business
customer service

In the mid-1880s, Benjamin Holt invented the Link-Belt Combined Harvester, which eventually became known as the Caterpillar tractor.[15] That invention led to the formation of the world's largest equipment and power systems company, still called Caterpillar, Inc., often referred to as "Cat" for short. With its roots in the invention of these powerful machines, Benjamin Holt's heirs today run an organization called Holt Cat. Holt Cat is the largest dealer of Caterpillar equipment in the United States. Headquartered in San Antonio, Texas, Holt Cat serves 118 counties across Texas and is led by CEO Peter M. Holt, great-grandson of Benjamin Holt. A hundred years after that first invention, Peter Holt saw the need to develop a long-term vision for his dealership. Working with management consultant Ken Blanchard, Holt adopted a values-based leadership model to move the company forward. Putting forth a vision, mission, and value statements for the entire world to see was a radical step in the construction industry. It was a way of boldly signaling to customers, employees, and suppliers that Holt was not just about profit. The company was announcing its plans to serve the customer with integrity and excellence.

According to Larry Mills, executive vice president of Holt Companies, "Our entire process defines success in terms of leading by a set of deeply held ethical values. This is in contrast to business as usual, where success is often defined only by size and profit. Our model says our whole community—employees, customers, shareholders and other stakeholders—will directly benefit from association with a company committed to doing the right thing."[16]

One of the driving principles at Holt Cat is to make sure that the Power of Yes works every day. Dave Harris, executive vice president and general manager of the dealership, calls it "concierge service." What does concierge service look like? "It's always going the extra mile," Harris explains. He says it starts by asking really good questions: "Our mission is clear: to provide legendary service for our customers. Our customers know what they are trying to accomplish. I think our job comes down to asking the right questions to help them find the right solution."[17]

Holt Cat people on the front end, whether sales or service, are taught to never assume they know more than their customers. Harris says the moment you think you know more than the customer does, everything changes. "We can tell our people to walk in our customer's shoes, but the truth is we can't. We have to really listen to them first and foremost. That's how we gain the insight to keep driving the business forward. We have to solve the problems they really have, not just try to sell them machines we have sitting on our yard. It's really a partnership."[18]

The company decided to expand its customer engagement strategy of saying yes by launching a new kind of customer support center. After eighty years in business, Holt is attempting to go where most dealerships haven't gone before by dramatically improving customer communications. Edward Craner, vice president of strategy and marketing, said, "To increase transparency and cut out red tape, we created the Sales Support Center to make it easier for current or prospective customers to get in touch with the right Holt person across the company. Instead of wasting customers' valuable time looking for answers to mundane questions about their equipment, parts and warranty, we'll do it for them."[19] Holt wants to throw out the rulebook that naturally evolves in legacy companies. Craner should know. He's a veteran of AT&T. "All that corporate red tape is designed to make *our* lives easier, not the customers'. Today they need much more personalized experiences and problem solving. That's what we are working towards becoming: even more of a high-touch kind of business."[20]

Most of Holt's customers are literally digging in the dirt somewhere in their territory. That means machines often break down, even the powerful Caterpillar equipment called "yellow iron" in recognition of the signature Cat color. The company stocks nearly a quarter of a million different parts for the varieties of Cat equipment they sell and service. But, many of the company's customers are working in remote parts of the state, so Holt created a Parts Express delivery system. It delivers over 98 percent of ordered parts overnight to 180 strategically located parts pickup locations, in nearly every county it serves. Cat's Parts Express trucks travel more than 6,500 miles a day to say "yes" to customers.[21]

Harris says that Holt has a reputation with its customers for not "beating around the bush." Holt encourages local management teams to solve customer problems as soon as possible. In the construction business, time is money. Often, contractors face large liquidated damages for job delays.

Holt is also in the power systems business. It sells and rents power-generating equipment that customers of all types use for primary or backup power. John, a loyal Holt customer, is a Texas-based concert promoter who travels internationally with major shows like the Trans-Siberian Orchestra. He says, "A lot of companies just rent you the generator. They fail to understand that I cannot afford any kind of an outage during a show. Between the lights and instruments, we are talking hundreds of thousands of dollars in equipment that can blow with one surge. My guys at Holt grasp that and go the extra mile to prevent it from happening. My only regret is that I can't take them with me around the country."

In an effort to continually remind their customers of the company's desire to serve them, Holt created a marketing campaign called "Let's Partner Up." The campaign is used throughout the company as part of its internal brand training. Every Holt team member is a "Let's Partner Up" brand ambassador. Members look for every opportunity to thank their customers for their business. Harris said, "We know who pays the bills. They honor us with their business. And that's what keeps us going."[22]

Profiting from the Power of Yes

When we look at the reasons that companies like Discount Tire, Châteauform', and Holt Cat have succeeded, it's not that complicated. They consistently look at their businesses from the customer's point of view. Then they figure out ways to empower their frontline people to stop saying no. This kind of thinking starts at the top. We see that in the attitudes of Bruce Halle, Jacques Horvitz, and Peter Holt. They practice no "no."

These companies profit handsomely by earning their customers' loyalty. But delivering on the Power of Yes takes much more than thinking it's a good idea. It means telling the truth. Frankly, it's why so many companies cannot say yes. They are shading the truth or making excuses to the customer. Everyone screws up occasionally, even Discount, Châteauform', and Holt. But the difference is, these companies own up to mistakes as part of their Customer CEO culture. These companies tell their customers the truth. Customers are either there to be manipulated for more money or they are seen as the reason for your existence. It can't be both. I challenge you to start thinking about your opportunities to quit saying no and start saying yes. Yes organizations are healthier and build more sustainable businesses. Saying yes makes a lot of sense.

Yes Companies Go Viral

Saying yes is contagious. You can't keep this attitude locked up in the attic. It welcomes the sunlight. Your people are waiting for permission to not say no, like the staff at the Mandarin Oriental Hotel Group. Once customers begin to understand this change, they keep coming back for more. Look at Discount Tire. By fixing flats as a gift, the company gives customers lifetime value that is significantly higher than that offered by its competitors.

Yes Companies Keep Getting Better

Innovation really means incremental improvement. It does not have to be a momentous jump forward; it can be small, incremental changes that improve the customer experience. Being a customer-focused organization requires continuous listening to customer demands and feedback. We see this at Châteauform', which constantly seeks ways to stretch itself as a company. Management isn't arrogant enough to believe that all the good ideas come from within. Here's a secret: sometimes the best ideas come from *without*, meaning from your customers.

Yes Companies Say "Power to the People"

It's everyone's job to say yes. Why does this seem so radical? Is it because we love to make rules and regulations to control our employees? The truth is, you restrict the happiness of your employees and your customers by not shifting more power to your people. At Holt, hundreds of field technicians go out into the field every day to face difficult situations with customers who can be openly hostile because they aren't making money with equipment that's down. The company has empowered its techs to make the call about what needs to happen, because they are in a position to know what's best.

Yes Companies Chase Customers, Not Profit

Why are you in business? Is it only to maximize your profit? Companies that chase profits at the expense of serving customers are in for a rude awakening. Today's customer is savvy about getting taken advantage of by companies that put their own interests first. Discount Tire could easily charge $20 to fix a flat. With six thousand opportunities to do that a day, the company might be leaving upwards of $40 million a year on the table. But that's not the way to look at it. How many tires will Discount Tire sell those same people over a lifetime? Chase your customers and say yes.

Yes Companies Live Their Values

Like Larry Mills at Holt Cat told me, "Of course, you have to have values in order to live them." Companies like Holt have revolutionized themselves and their industries by putting their values right up front for everyone to see. It's a way to be willing to have a report card of your intent and performance. You won't always get it right. Values are aspirational. But, Customer CEOs expect no less. They will reward you for your efforts because you are showing you are willing to be held accountable.

Yes Companies Let Their People Break the Rules

Nothing is more important to succeeding at the Power of Yes. The old saying, "Break the rules and ask permission later" wouldn't be needed if companies just trusted their own people to do the right thing. Maybe you should just have fewer rules. But, if that's not possible, encourage a culture of rule breaking whenever it benefits the customer. Guess what? Customers sometimes lie. But if you look at it as a cost of doing business, it will frustrate you a lot less and it will keep customers coming back. Imagine how many other people they will tell.

Yes Is Only One Letter More Than No

Maybe it's easier to keep saying no because the word is so short. Becoming a yes company starts by simply practicing saying the word. Try it. You will find that your people and your customers will begin to think about your company in an entirely different light. The Customer CEO is waiting for you to start.

(How well does your organization engage the Power of Yes? Visit customerceopowercheck.com to download our free diagnostic tool.)

9

The Power of the Platform

Key Customer CEO Question:

What about my ideas?

In the good old days, if you had a bad meal at a restaurant you might complain to the manager and seek a reduction in your bill or, more likely, just never return. Maybe the next day you'd tell a few coworkers about your miserable experience. I call a customer experience disaster like this a Fawlty Fiasco. "Fawlty" refers to comedian John Cleese's classic British television show, *Fawlty Towers*. The innkeeper character he played, Basil Fawlty, was a bumbling, sarcastic, and generally lazy business owner who loathed his customers.

Fawlty Towers was the opposite of a Customer CEO establishment. The program featured extraordinarily unhappy customers in every episode. In "Waldorf Salad," Fawlty met his match with an aggressive American business executive, Mr. Hamilton, who simply wanted to order a Waldorf salad.[1] Fawlty and Hamilton nearly come to blows over the proper ingredients for the salad (which are, by the way, celery, apples, walnuts, and grapes, topped with mayonnaise). Hamilton berates Fawlty, calling him "the British Tourist Board's answer to Donald Duck." Just imagine what he might have said about Fawlty Towers if he'd had access to Twitter.

As customers, we've all seen our share of Fawlty Fiascos. As businesspeople in the Customer CEO era, we have to begin seriously reconsidering how to engage our current and future customers. The Mr. Hamiltons of today can crucify any business, whether that business deserves it or not. You can't underestimate the power of an angry customer. The statistics are overwhelming: an unhappy customer will let twelve people know about his bad experience. Those twelve will tell six more. Those six will tell three of their friends and, voilà, your single Fawlty Fiasco will have been shared with almost four hundred people. Today, social media platforms can magnify that number exponentially. It seems that William Shakespeare was prophetic when he wrote, "All the world's a stage." Everyone carries a phone that has become both a tool and a weapon. People text and they tweet. They shoot photos and post videos. As you are reading these words, millions of strangers around the world could play a role in the success or failure of your enterprise. If you aren't listening, you'll never know what hit you.

This social generation has become judge, jury, and executioner of businesses that don't operate the way customers think they should. Many of you businesspeople are reluctant participants in this new social commerce. Like anything else that's new and uncertain, the initial response is that maybe, just maybe, this is a fad that will soon pass, and things will go back to normal. But, as with every other information revolution, the changes are here to stay; we will never return to the way things used to be. Successful businesses will be the ones that have the vision and the stamina to push forward through the fog of the platform.

The platform is everywhere. Between computers, laptops,

mobile devices, interactive televisions, and gaming platforms, wherever people are they have digital soapboxes. Some companies see the platform as a place to collect, crunch, and coalesce the collective comments and actions of their customers. With enough data, many believe they can even predict the future with artificial intelligence algorithms.

Katherine Losse, a longtime Facebook executive, explained how pervasive the platform has become. "You can't get away from it. It's everything. It's everywhere. The moment we're in now is about trying to deal with all this technology rather than rejecting it, because obviously we can't reject it entirely."[2]

Real-Time Engagement

If customers have embraced the platform, it is up to smart businesses to understand why. By directly engaging with them in a straightforward manner, you will profit in many important ways, none more important than innovation. If you turn the platform into a proactive feedback machine, you can tap into a steady stream of fresh thinking and new ideas about product and service improvements as well as the enhanced experiences that deliver them. Believe it or not, you can also understand in real time what the customer is experiencing with your brand, from her initial marketing impression to purchase. The platform is innovation.

What is innovation really? It is improving something that already is, not creating something new. New creation is invention. Alexander Graham Bell invented the telephone; Steve Jobs innovated with the iPhone. Everything, no matter how mundane, can be improved to benefit customers. For instance, everyone who has ever flown has used the ordinary airline boarding pass. It's just some information printed on paper that ends up being discarded millions of times a day. Passengers just accept what is spit out of a check-in kiosk or what they print from their computers before heading to the airport. From the passenger's point of view, a boarding pass should have, at a minimum, the flight number, the gate, the seat number, and the boarding time. But, if you are like me, you might have trouble actually reading one as you are rushing down a dimly lit airport concourse.

After graphic designer Tyler Thompson became frustrated with a hard-to-read boarding pass, he created the Boarding Pass Fail blog both to vent and to create an open forum for like-minded designers to create better solutions. Thompson wrote about the plight of most passengers in the voice of an airline: "You're confused, lost, and just want to get on your flight, it's cool we don't really care, and we sure as hell don't want to make this process easy and enjoyable for you. Instead we hired a small, blind parakeet to lay out your boarding pass, you know, just to keep you guessing. Have fun."[3] Thompson and a host of other designers took it upon themselves to design boarding passes that were easier to read, with clearer layouts, larger fonts, and better color palettes. Thompson's innovation was developed to solve a specific set of customer problems. It proves that even the most ordinary item has the potential to be improved if you just look at it through fresh eyes.

But, sadly, airlines are particularly bad about listening to their customers, much less looking for innovative ideas from them about how to improve the customer experience. Take Dave Carroll as an example. Who's Dave Carroll? He's the Canadian musician who decided to tell the world about United Airlines destroying his guitar. I can think of no better example of a real life "David versus Goliath on the platform" than Dave Carroll. After getting zero satisfaction from United, he wrote a song, shot a video, and posted it to YouTube.[4] "United Breaks Guitar" went viral and became an instant hit. It had more than twelve million views. Carroll sang, "You broke it and should fix it, you might as well admit it, I should have flown with someone else or gone by car, 'cause United breaks guitars."

Of course, United Airlines isn't the only company that doesn't understand the Power of the Platform. Progressive Insurance's brand was damaged in a controversial case in which the company refused to pay the claim of a deceased policyholder. The brother of the deceased posted an epic rant about the company called

"My Sister Paid Progressive Insurance to Defend Her Killer in Court."[5] The company reacted badly, with insensitive public relations spin. The platform pushed back. Even after the company and family settled, angered people continued to post scathing comments like this on Progressive's Facebook page: "Hey look at that, you agreed to pay off the claim the family was originally entitled to. All it took was losing a trial, a media firestorm, and the impending loss of countless customers."

It's stories like these that make a lot of executives cringe and defer meaningful discussions about understanding and engaging the Power of the Platform. When I work with companies, I continue to hear the same eight reasons from leadership about why paying attention to the platform is not worth the time and investment.

- It's a fad
- There's no return on investment
- It will only damage our brand's reputation
- The company lacks time or resources to do it right
- We can't control the message
- We're afraid of making mistakes
- Our staff lacks experience
- We don't really care about what they are saying

In his book *The Now Revolution*, author Jay Baer explained how things have changed:

If a customer had a problem with a company, she would send a letter or an e-mail, or perhaps she would call a toll-free number. The company would hear the customer's complaint, consider its merits, and take an action in response. That action was often less than immediate. In the case of mailed complaint letters, receiving a response from a company in thirty days or more wasn't considered unusual or unresponsive. And all of these interactions took place in private. Not anymore.[6]

This slow response and often outright indifference has created pent-up demand for a platform that lets customers "get even" and balance the power. The good news is that more companies are changing their attitudes about what's happening on the platform, including clothing retailer L.L.Bean. The company noticed that a popular fitted sheet was getting many negative online reviews, so it decided to remove the sheets from the website until it learned the cause of the problem. The vendor had made a manufacturing mistake that was causing the fabric to fail. L.L.Bean's chief marketing officer Steve Fuller said, "Before, it would have taken us months and months to figure out if something was wrong with the product through returns, if we ever would have known at all."[7]

This platform represents two major opportunities for companies. First, by closely listening to and engaging with people, you can gain hundreds of fresh insights that you can use for improving your brand's marketing and customer service, not to mention improved product ideas. Second, you can enhance the customer experience by being transparent and hearing the criticism. Unfortunately, for too many companies the temptation is to just talk the talk. These companies prefer to focus on what they are selling versus what the customer really needs or thinks.

The Wide World of Big Data

We now live in a big data world. IBM defines big data this way: "Every day, we create 2.5 quintillion bytes of data—so much that 90% of the data in the world today has been created in the last two years alone. This data comes from everywhere: sensors used to gather climate information, posts to social media sites, digital pictures and videos, purchase transaction records, and cell phone GPS signals to name a few. This data is big data."[8] And it keeps growing at an alarming and unprecedented rate.

Consulting firm Deloitte reported that by the end of 2012, more than 90 percent of the Fortune 500 will have launched big data programs.[9] At the macro level, this means that companies are investing billions of dollars to gain a better understanding of their customers the big data way. Big data can reveal previously unseen patterns that can help companies deliver higher levels of performance.

Paul Pellman is CEO of Adometry, an advertising attribution technology and analytics firm. The company provides deeper insight into the overall performance and incremental ROI of online cross-channel marketing efforts by crunching billions of pieces of data. Pellman says, "The question we hear from companies all the time is 'how do we make sense of it all?' It's as if all the data have created a kind of fog that's shrouding good decision-making. But the solution is not having less data; it's getting your hands on the right tools to make sense of it all. Companies need to begin turning their data from just something to warehouse into actionable insight."[10]

Customer relationship management (CRM) is an essential strategic business tool for tracking and managing current and future customer relationships. By combining business processes and technology, companies can focus on building their businesses. By discovering more about customer behavior, you can make better decisions in the areas of sales, marketing, and customer service. With online platforms like salesforce.com, every company, no matter the size, can be up and running with easy-to-use interfaces and dashboards. This is a necessary, and time-saving, technology.

Just because you can collect customer data, however, doesn't mean it's a good idea to do it. It turns out that many customers are squeamish about handing over too much control of their lives to any entity, even the brands they trust. There are legitimate privacy concerns. As one recent customer I interviewed said, "Big Data sounds too much like Big Brother." There is growing discomfort with the way companies like Google and Facebook are using the data they have collected from their users.

David "Doc" Searls, author of *The Intention Economy: When Customers Take Charge*, supports a growing trend to turn away from a complete dependence on big data. He says that many customers are disabling data collection sites. He sees an inevitable trend toward vendor relationship management; think CRM in reverse, a system in which customers stay in control of their vital information. Searls sees a future where "demand finds supply," with personal requests for proposals (RFPs) sent by customers to vendors. "Your personal RFP is an event that triggers rules" that dictate the types of information a customer is willing to share and with whom.[11]

No doubt, this is a brave new world. The key questions you must ask yourself are: Does any of this data bring us closer to understanding the Customer CEO? Does it improve our customers' experience? Does it help us sell more effectively and efficiently? Or is it just a new way to try to sell people more stuff they don't actually need? Don't get me wrong. I am not anti-data. To the contrary, I believe in it when it is used responsibly. I founded two web data companies and have seen the power of data when it's viewed as a tool to make better business decisions.

The solution is to begin to rethink your business and to tap every employee as a kind of "listening post" who's plugged into the ongoing, 24–7 customer conversation. Social media expert Steve Patti explains that this starts with utilizing some simple tools:

> Social media monitoring is a discipline that is still in its infancy in terms of tools, techniques, and being embraced by organizations. While social media is often categorized as a collection of marketing engagement channels—it is really a collection of corporate engagement channels. There are multiple types of conversations going on at any one time online—and those conversations can provide organizations with a glimpse into a range of insights: brand perception, product feedback, channel preferences, product ease of use, service delivery, support and warranty, etc. Customers will share things with friends or professional colleagues on social sites that they won't share in primary research.[12]

Social media are only a set of tools, not a panacea. They offer a way to listen and communicate that can give you surface-level information. Individual human beings want to be seen and heard as individuals. They can be a major source of innovation for you, if you are willing to listen. Let's take a look at how a few companies are using the Power of the Platform to innovate in the age of the Customer CEO.

The Greatest Customer Service Story Ever Told

Hey @Mortons—can you meet me at newark airport with a porterhouse when land in two hours? K, thanks. :)
Tweet from a passenger sitting on a plane before leaving the gate

If you want to really understand the Power of the Platform, let's review what happened late one afternoon in Newark, New Jersey. What started as a spur-of-the-moment joke became the gold standard for customer treatment by a company that was *really* listening and got it right.

Author, blogger, and angel investor Peter Shankman was running behind all day and all he could think about was how hungry he was as he headed to Newark. Shankman loves Morton's Steakhouse and is a regular customer. Morton's is an upscale steak house serving a business clientele since 1969. The business has grown to more than seventy restaurants, with locations around the world. Shankman had no expectations that anyone at Morton's would even read his tweet, much less act on it. "Let's understand: I was joking. I had absolutely no expectations of anything from that tweet. It's like how we tweet 'Dear Winter, please stop, love Peter,' or something similar."[13]

Two and a half hours later, Shankman was stunned to find a Morton's employee waiting for him in the terminal with a twenty-four-ounce porterhouse steak, an order of shrimp, side orders, and flatware. Someone at Morton's corporate had seen the tweet and set a plan in motion. A tuxedoed employee was dispatched with the meal from Morton's in Hackensack, New Jersey, over twenty miles from Newark. Logistically, this took a lot of effort, with no guarantee that the employee bearing the food would arrive in time to intercept Shankman before he left the airport.

How many companies would jump through those kinds of hoops to actually do this? Shankman wrote, "I have no doubt that countless companies think like that. They think along the lines of 'Oh, too many logistics. That'll never work,' and they leave it at that. But what if it *does work?* What if it happens, and it works *perfectly*, and it shocks the living hell out of the person they do it to? Like it did tonight?"[14]

What Morton's has done through deeper listening is innovate the customer experience it delivers. Perhaps jumping through hoops to meet a passenger with a hot meal at an airport is an extreme example, but how many opportunities are there for every company? The key is to be ready to leap into action to show customers what they mean to you. They will do the rest by spreading the word far and wide about your willingness to go the extra mile.

This is an important story for another reason. Shankman makes a persuasive case for frontline empowerment. He wrote, "Stay on top of what people are saying about you. Respond accordingly. Perhaps most importantly, have a chain of command in place that actually *lets* you do these things in real time. Had Morton's had to get permission to make this happen, at 5:10pm on a Wednesday night, there's no way it ever would have."[15]

But, enough about just listening to customers' ideas. What if you based your entire business model on delivering exceptional value exclusively from the platform?

Now Everyone's an Inventor

When I first got the idea for my new kind of scissors, it was by observing people who had difficulty holding a traditional pair in their hands. It was so simple to me. That was the easy part. The killer was the process of getting the IP and building real *prototypes. It was more than $150,000 and that ruled me out because I can't get that kind of money.*

John, Chicago, Illinois
Participant in a customer interview about entrepreneurship

I have heard variations of John's story many times throughout my career. As an entrepreneur, I have always looked for other people who have both killer ideas that can improve people's lives and a business model that will deliver financial success. It is very difficult for the everyday inventor to find the backing he needs to launch a new product, no matter how great a solution he came up with. Usually, friends and family money is tapped out. Venture capitalists and private equity firms want more scale and management expertise than these entrepreneurs generally have. Angel investors today demand more sophistication as well. So now we have Quirky.

Quirky.com was created as an end-to-end product design company for the "little guy." Its website explains, "For centuries, becoming an 'inventor' has been a hard gig to crack. Complexities relating to financing, engineering, distribution, and legalities have stood in the way of brilliant people executing on their great ideas."[16] Founder Ben Kaufman was the wunderkind behind the company. He knew that the old model was broken: people needed a platform where their ideas were welcome. "We're making invention accessible," he told *Entrepreneur* magazine. "Ninety-nine percent of people are armchair inventors. They have great product ideas, but most don't have the time or money or expertise to make them happen."[17]

Imagine an online community of over 250,000 members with hundreds of new creations showing up each week from "ideators." Here are some recent candidates posted to the site.

- An ironing station that replaces your wall-mounted ironing board
- Smartphone-enabled bicycle signal lights—turn signal lights activate via smart phone application and GPS built into the phone

- Bed bug killing bags, which would contain and kill any bedbugs you might pick up in your travels
- An iPod/iPad/iPhone charging case, which is charged and then can charge your iPod on the go

Quirky is crowdsourcing gone wild. Anybody can join in and bring her idea to the platform. The community helps better define, shape, and refine the offerings. There's a voting system in place so that the most market-worthy products advance. When there's a consensus that a product is market ready, Quirky's staff goes to work getting the product manufactured, packaged, and ready to sell. The company has created nearly two hundred partnerships with a variety of major retailers, including Bed Bath & Beyond, Target, Toys "R" Us, The Container Store, Amazon, and OfficeMax. Quirky offers its inventors an attractive revenue-sharing model that is profitable for both.

Frank Piller, a director of the Smart Customization Group at the Massachusetts Institute of Technology, said that Kaufman has created "the next step in retail co-creation," looking at Quirky as a fusion of small inventor and retail marketplace. "There are companies that take ideas from customers, but very few go a step further and put products on the market that really involve customers in all stages of the value chain," according to Piller.[18]

Steal a page from Quirky. Many of your customers have big ideas as well. They want to cocreate and collaborate with the companies with which they do business. They may have plenty of useful ideas about how to improve both the form and the function of your products. Why not create a listening space using today's social tools to turn your customers into "partners" like Quirky is doing?

Mobile Research in Real Time

It's frustrating. The problem with typical market research methods is that the information is already outdated by the time we get the report back. I would like to be able to respond to my customers

much faster. They have so many great ideas we need to under-
stand or I fear losing them. We need something that's real time.
Amy, St. Louis, Missouri
Participant in interview, chief marketing officer

Fiona Blades shared Amy's frustrations. After nearly twenty years as a marketing manager and an advertising agency account planner, Blades saw the problem getting worse, not better. Traditional market research methodologies had always lacked certainty and clarity. Whether she was using customer surveys, focus groups, or one-on-one interviews, Blades saw a glaring flaw: people just forget. They are leading busy lives, and they often had great difficulty remembering why they might have chosen a certain product over another. Even worse, they rarely could recall where they had heard the message about a particular product or service. It's tough to recommend a media campaign strategy for a client if you don't really know what is connecting with the customer.

An even bigger question concerned the ability to accurately understand the real steps customers were taking in their journey from consideration to purchase. Blades said, "When I thought about this I realized this went back a long way. In 1997, I came up with the idea of the Brand Experience Workshop for the agency I was working with at the time. Rather than think about a Brand Essence, I thought it was important to assess the Brand Experience over time. So we created a Brand Experience Score that enabled us to 'play' up different elements to different target audiences through different media."[19]

In 2001, Blades pitched for the World Cup promotion for a soft drink manufacturer her agency represented. She proposed using texting as an integral part of the campaign. The promotion asked customers to text whenever they had a soft drink, so the company could see where they were, what they were doing, and whom they were with. Five years later, Blades founded MESH Planning to focus on what she was now calling Real-time Experience Tracking (RET). I asked Blades about the inspiration for RET, and she shared this insight:

I saw we could really crack the problem of how to evaluate integrated marketing activity. The mobile phone held the answer. When we started in 2006 we believed that Real-time Experience Tracking was a better solution to help track marketing campaigns because we picked up every aspect from the TV ad to social media and we could provide rapid feedback so that campaigns could be optimized as they rolled out. However, we have heard clients needing to understand the path to purchase better. New teams are being built to focus on the shopper. New research is needed to help these teams and we have found that picking up experiences in real-time can help here too. By listening to customers we can create our innovation road map."

MESH teamed with Emma Macdonald and Hugh Wilson of Cranfield University, located north of London, to help understand the true impact of RET. They had analyzed and interpreted nearly a million company–customer interactions. These touch points have spanned several leading industries, including financial services, entertainment, electronics, and consumer beverages. In an article for the *Harvard Business Review*, Macdonald and Wilson wrote, "And because RET enables companies to assess and respond in real time to customers' reactions to products, services or branding efforts, it can play a central role in allowing customers to help design their own experiences with products."[20]

A typical RET study asks a panel of customers or prospects to "report in" via text message on every connection with a specific brand or its competitors for a period ranging from a week to a month. The customer is not aware of who the actual client is. Blades explained that, "We want our brand clients to understand their customers better. Participants actively engage with us. We empower them by asking them to tell us when they come across relevant experiences. We provide them with the tools—a texting framework and an online diary. They can upload photos of the experiences and provide more detailed comments in their own words."

Mobile technology is transforming marketing for brands. MESH clients like LG Electronics, Pepsi, and Unilever are learning much more about their customers' experiences than they have previously known. For example, LG Electronics is seeking to become a major player in the U.S. home electronics and appliances market. Using RET since the beginning of 2010, LG has gained unique insight into every touch point along the customer experience journey. LG has been able to reallocate its marketing investments "on the fly" with the real-time feedback the company is getting.

Blades is excited about the innovation that the Power of the Platform is providing:

> I see many opportunities for RET. The fundamental change in marketing, with its shift in power toward people and away from companies, is exciting. However good the customers' thoughts are about innovation, it needs the company to pick these up and run with them. Companies set up to do this will succeed. Those that aren't will become increasingly out of touch with their customers and their brands will answer fewer and fewer needs.

Fiona Blades' advice to every brand is simple. "Listen. Then cocreate. That's innovation."

Profiting from the Platform

Customers today are empowered and they're on the march. Social technology is turning into social commerce. The problem for many companies is that the customer is often way ahead of the curve. Customer CEO companies will be recognized for their ability to engage in active, social listening. Customers will increasingly expect no less from the brands they choose to support. It should be clear to you by now that no matter what you say or do to prevent it, today's customer is in control, particularly online. These customers will act and react about what you do or don't do, independent of your input. You cannot eliminate the negative, but you can design a platform strategy that openly encourages an authentic conversation. You will profit by becoming a true listening post on the front line and online as we've seen through the examples of Morton's, Quirky, and MESH Planning.

Today's customers are online and connected. They expect, and in some cases demand, that their voices be heard. This means that it is absolutely essential for you to adopt some kind of proactive listening program. Today's technology means it is easier than ever before to see real-time positive and negative feedback from your customers throughout the entire purchase consideration/sales cycle.

But there is a big disconnect between what company leaders say and what customers actually experience. We hear a steady refrain from CEOs about their dedication to putting customers first. Yet according to some of the stories, customer service in some quarters is worse than ever. Rather than help move customers from pain to gain, some companies seem to be locked in a race to the bottom. While big data can help you see patterns in customer demographics and behavior, you cannot rely on big data completely to tell you what your customers want; big data is the "what." It is essential to ask "why" through insight research. As you move forward, keep the following key points in mind.

One Letter Can Change Everything

I want to present you with a simple idea that will help you understand the Power of the Platform. By changing just one letter in a word, you can transform your business. By turning your company into a 360-degree listening post, you will no longer be a place of *killeD* ideas. You will be transformed into a place of *killeR* ideas. Remove the D and replace it with an R. That's what the platform will do for you.

The Platform Is a New Form of Service

Customer CEO companies know they exist to serve their customers. This is the heart of the matter. They value this truth more than anything; it isn't just lip service for a press release or a short-term sales promotion. It is a philosophy, a higher calling. Morton's didn't *have to* meet Peter Shankman at the Newark Airport with a porterhouse steak. The company wanted to do it. And, give Morton's credit for seeing a marketing opportunity that has put the restaurant light-years ahead of its competition. If you Google "greatest customer service story ever," you will find this story at the top of the page. What company wouldn't want that?

Let Your Customers Bring Innovation to You

As we saw with Quirky, people are looking for places to plug in their ideas. Quirky has provided a platform for inventors, but what about your customers who have fresh ideas about your products and services? Are you open to the idea of partnering with them for their help? You can create win–win opportunities and become known as a collaborative brand willing to actively engage with customers.

This Is Hard Work

Don't be fooled by social media gurus who tell you how easy it is to engage with the plartform. It is not. Understanding and embracing the Power of the Platform is not some simple fix, learned in a half-day seminar. Books or blogs that list "twenty-one essential social media things to do" are probably wrong for your company. That's because every company is unique. Your culture must embrace and apply the methods of outstanding customer engagement that work best for you. Stay in the game and keep building your capabilities. What worked for L.L.Bean was different from what worked for Morton's. MESH's real-time experience tracking requires companies to think differently about interacting with customers. But the payoff will be worth it.

Shift Responsibility to Frontline Employees

Who knows your customers better than the employees in your stores and contact centers? You trust them to represent your brand. So shift more responsibility to them and provide them with real-time information. Loosen rules and let them fix problems now, not later, based on the input they are getting from customers. You may never get another chance, so don't cut costs in this vital area of the business.

Balance Big Data with Human Connection

Getting your arms around big data is complicated. The volume of data won't slow down, and it increases exponentially each year. You can't rely on big data exclusively. Make a renewed commitment to spend time listening to people through all of your channels.

The Power of the Platform Is Explosive

The Power of the Platform is dynamic—and dangerous—for everybody. The rules are being written and rewritten every day. The sooner you proactively embrace the platform, the faster you will begin to understand it. Think of the changes in this arena as a giant wave that is building to a crest. You want to be riding the wave, not being crushed under the sheer weight of the water. This is not the time to play defense. The Customer CEO holds the Power of the Platform in her hands and won't give it back. Your competitors aren't waiting; what are you waiting for?

(How well does your organization engage the Power of the Platform? Visit customerceopowercheck.com to download our free diagnostic tool.)

10

The Power of Rebellion

Key Customer CEO Question:

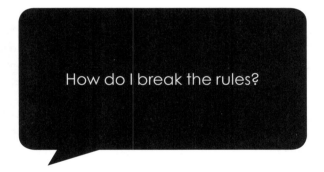

How do I break the rules?

Controversy is no stranger to actor Alec Baldwin. When an American Airlines flight attendant asked him to turn his phone off shortly before departing Los Angeles, the fireworks started.[1] Baldwin refused to comply with the flight attendant's request and was removed from the aircraft. He tweeted: "Flight attendant on American reamed me out 4 playing WORDS W FRIENDS while we sat at the gate, not moving. #nowonderamericaairisbankrupt."

American Airlines' Facebook page reported the incident this way:

The passenger ultimately stood up (with the seat belt light still on for departure) and took his phone into the plane's lavatory. He slammed the lavatory door so hard, the cockpit crew heard it and became alarmed, even with the cockpit door closed and locked...the passenger was extremely rude to the crew, calling them inappropriate names and using offensive language. Given the facts above, the passenger was removed from the flight and denied boarding.

If you have flown on a commercial jet anytime during the mobile phone era, you are familiar with the ban on use once the door to the plane is closed. Even if you are a rich and famous television star like Baldwin, there should be no surprises. Those are the rules, no ifs, ands, or buts. Of course, airlines love their rules. A few years ago, a simple ninety-minute nonstop flight I took turned into a nine-hour adventure as the plane variously landed, took off, taxied, waited, and refueled at three airports due to inclement weather in Atlanta. Being a safety-first kind of guy, that made sense. What didn't were the bizarre explanations we got along the way because of an intricate combination of rules by Delta Airlines, the airports, and the Federal Aviation Administration. Our lives are run by someone else's rules, no matter how ridiculous they may seem.

If you are honest, whether you approve of Baldwin's antics or not, his act of rebellion may resonate with you, especially if you tend to be a rule follower. Don't misunderstand: rules are important in a civil society. But when faced with seemingly pointless decrees, you may have rebelled in some small way yourself by refusing to turn your phone all the way off, just to spite a pompous flight attendant. This is about control and conformity. People resent the show of power by organizations, particularly if they believe the rules are unfair or unnecessary. My research over the years has shown that customers resent being taken for granted or treated like children.

Perhaps you remember the old-style Walgreen's drug stores.

For many years customers could only enter the store through a metal turnstile. Once inside, they were forced to navigate a byzantine path leading through every aisle in the store before they could escape. There was no doubt who was in control, and it certainly wasn't the customer. Those old-style stores were more like prisons than pharmacies. Someone finally figured that out, and a modern Walgreen's is a pleasant experience. Even in this social age, corporations of every size, in every industry, still march forward every day creating new rules that serve as barriers to entry for customers. They spend billions of dollars every year teaching their people the rules and how to enforce them. Why not stop the madness and let customers rebel on purpose?

A few years ago, I created a television campaign for a regional wireless company called Pocket Communications. Our research had shown that people were sick and tired of long-term contracts and fine print that always favored the company. So Pocket created a no-contract, low-cost business model. The commercials featured a chimpanzee, portraying the average customer, rebelling against the "big cell company." In one spot, our chimp hero waits patiently and finally presents the store manager with his forty- or fifty-page bill. The manager carefully explains, using a magnifying glass, that the fine print says that the company has every right to add every possible charge known to man or monkey. Of course, our hero goes crazy and destroys the store in a sheer display of "I'm as mad as hell and I can't take it anymore!"

Someone who understands this frustration with rule culture is Renee Fannin, owner of Napa Valley Toy Company, who owns three retail locations in Northern California. While I was walking past her store on Main Street in downtown Napa, I noticed that she had posted "Rules" on the store's front door. Wondering what kind of terrible transgressions the children of Napa had committed in the store, I was intrigued. The hand-lettered sign read:

1. No being mean in the store.
2. No negative comments about anything.

3. No saying "Target," "Wal-Mart," or "Amazon/online."
4. No complaining or saying "we have too many Legos, yo-yos, etc."
5. If your mom, dad, grandma, grandpa, aunt, uncle, friend, nanny buy you something say "thanks."

People hate rules. The more there are, the more they want to break them. They also resent it when they feel that rules are unfairly applied. If you must have rules, couldn't they be more fun, like Napa Valley Toys' rules? Customers love companies that don't take themselves too seriously. You can engage customers by adding sheer joy to your business, and you will profit by making that a competitive advantage for your company. Honestly, it's easy to win at this game because so few companies commit themselves to engaging customers through the Power of Rebellion.

The Star of the Waltz

I won't go to a symphony. My mom dragged me there when I was a kid and it was a miserable experience. Who wants to listen to stuffy music written by a bunch of dead guys?

Tony, Nashville, Tennessee
Participant in a focus group about the symphony
and classical music

Is there any other business in the world where you pay for the privilege of having someone purposely turn his back to you? That only begins to describe the problems that symphonies around the world have faced over the past thirty years. Classical music has been the victim of a generational split around the world. As other music genres from rock to rap have captivated younger fans, the allure of the symphony has faded. To put it bluntly: What do you do when your audience is gradually dying off?

Even in Europe, where the symphony was born, it's been a

tough sell. Business strategy consultant Jason Hunter explains it this way:

> Look at the obstacles. If you were to even consider going to a performance, you have to pick an obscurely named symphony from composers deceased for hundreds of years. Even if you know of a particular symphony you would like to attend, there's little chance that your local symphony will be playing it when you would like to go, as they often develop their programs a year or more in advance. In the event you decide to attend a performance a series of obstacles face you. You'll need proper attire because that's the tradition. That can mean renting a gown or a tuxedo. You will need to hire a car or take a taxi so your formal clothes won't be ruined on public transportation. Once there, you will have little familiarity with the music, the composer, the conductor or any of the members of the symphony. It's hard to be a fan of the symphony in the modern world.[2]

This experience contrasts sharply with attending a rock concert, where you likely know intimate details about every member of the band. For most people under forty, attending the symphony can also be a culture shock. For example, at intermission they will be surrounded by much older "symphony elites," who speak in hushed tones about various obscure details of the performance. Worst of all, the overall performance is usually long and sleep inducing. This is not a winning formula; going to the symphony is expensive, unfamiliar, and boring.

But when the entire classical music industry saw despair, one man saw opportunity. Dutch classical violinist André Rieu has built his Johann Strauss Orchestra into a multimillion-dollar global empire, including sold-out stadium performances, CDs, videos, and television appearances. Rieu is so popular that he is ranked as the number-one male touring artist in the world of all music genres. The odds are that you have never heard of him. In fact, his own staff refers to him as the most popular unknown artist in the world.

Instead of rock star, Rieu is a waltz star. With his warm smile, magnetic stage presence, and flowing long hair he has mastered the Power of Rebellion by letting people break all the rules of the symphony. He performs at outdoor stadiums to sell-out crowds up to forty thousand. That's a long way from a typical symphony hall that might seat a maximum of two thousand. Instead of the formal symphony atmosphere, Rieu creates spectacles that include thousands of falling balloons, beautiful flowers, and colorfully costumed performers. His concerts often feature the unorthodox: one hundred bagpipers outfitted in kilts playing "Amazing Grace," horse-drawn Cinderella-style coaches, skating rinks, and sets that look like genuine castles. A typical André Rieu performance features more than 250 total performers, including a fifty-member orchestra. The production requires 250 support staff, eighty truckloads of sets, and twelve tons of sound equipment.[3] This is not your grandfather's symphony.

Imagine taking a virtually dead genre and reinventing it as something entertaining and fun. That's what people come to the concerts for: to be part of an epic experience, where thousands of strangers can share a joy-filled evening of music, color, humor, and entertainment. From a business point of view, Rieu carefully crafts his offering. He features more familiar—and shorter—musical pieces, mixing well-known waltzes, pop songs, and movie themes or, as he says, anything that touches the heart. His audiences are very casually dressed, which removes the stuffy symphony atmosphere. The large venues are an opportunity for audience participation, with sing-alongs, swaying, and dancing. Rieu said, "I want to give classical music back to the people, where it belongs. Mozart composed his music not for the elite, but for everybody. He was a fantastic, lively guy; he was drinking and having fun in life and being a genius at the same time."[4]

But why the waltz? Rieu says that to him, the waltz is much

more than just music. It's his way of connecting emotionally with his audience. "The waltz can be sad and at the same time uplifting. You have to see life from both sides, and the waltz encapsulates that. If you're in my audience you give yourself to me and the waltz will grab you," Rieu says.[5] Always the consummate showman, Rieu wants to touch everyone with his gift.

Leo Schofield, cofounder and creative director of Ovation, an Australian arts-based television network, explains Rieu's magnetic appeal. He says that nineteenth-century composers of waltzes and polkas, like Strauss, were really about providing fun for their audiences. Schofield believes Rieu is the modern-day Strauss. "It's easy to be snide about his popularity, but he's an absolutely perfect fit for the times...he's wholesome, projects a tremendous amiability, and you can see in his concerts that he believes his music is fun and should be fun for the audience too."[6]

Many classical music purists and critics are not big fans of Rieu's formula. I have used his story as a case study in workshops for a number of years, showing how even obscure industries can be turned around by gaining fresh insight from potential customers. Some people have complained that he doesn't understand the authentic classical music experience and that he is ruining the industry. Rieu's response is to smile all the way to the bank. According to *Billboard* magazine's 2011 top concert tours, Rieu ranked ninth in the world, with his 102 performances selling more than 650,000 tickets for an estimated $67 million.[7] He also sells hundreds of thousand of concert CDs and DVDs, as well as merchandise. It seems that giving people a way to break the rules can be extremely profitable.

The Most Interesting Beer in the World

He's like a mix of James Bond and Indiana Jones. He's a woman magnet. Who wouldn't want to be that guy?

David, Santa Monica, California
Participant in a focus group about beer

147

Ed Benfield has been listening to customers for a long time. In 1984 he conducted focus groups with beer drinkers in Huntsville, Alabama. Benfield says, "What we learned in Huntsville was earth-shattering. We got them talking about who drinks what beer. They told us that guys who drink regular beer are stupid, overweight, blowhard, insensitive jerks. That indicated—and we confirmed it over the next year or two—that light beer drinkers had begun to feel superior."[8] Benfield saw a great opportunity for the expansion of the light beer category and recommended that his client shift marketing resources to capture more of the coming market. He was right. Sales for light beer skyrocketed for the next twenty years.

Fast forward to 2006. In only a few years, Dos Equis, a low-volume Mexican import beer, transformed itself from an obscure regional brand into the sixth-largest imported beer sold in the United States. The brand's customer research had shown that the fraternity-house approach to marketing that had been a staple of beer advertising for decades was wearing thin. "Sophomoric humor has long been a category staple, and the majority of our competitors' advertising was insulting our consumer's intelligence. There was, and continues to be an opportunity for Dos Equis to stand out in the crowd by acknowledging and harnessing our consumer's thirst for intelligent humor," said Colin Westcott-Pitt, VP of marketing for Dos Equis.[9]

This insight led to the creation of "The Most Interesting Man in the World" campaign. The brand won a Gold Effie in 2009, a prestigious annual marketing communications award. The case study document for the campaign prepared by the brand's advertising agency, Euro RSCG, made the case for the big idea: "They [customers] felt misrepresented and misunderstood. Probing further, we discovered two important truths: First, what these guys wanted more than anything, more than hot girls and designer toys, was to be seen as interesting. And conversely, that they were terrified of being seen as boring. We sniffed an opportunity."[10]

In a series of more than thirty television commercials

produced by the brand's agency, we see an older gray-bearded man actively engaged in a variety of exotic, adventurous, and dangerous pursuits: running with the bulls, ski jumping, arm wrestling the police, releasing a grizzly bear from a trap, piloting a motorboat full of beauty-pageant winners. In one commercial the narrator tells us that, "His reputation is expanding faster than the universe. He once had an awkward moment just to see how it feels. He lives vicariously through himself. He is the most interesting man in the world." In the closing shot, we see this man seated, surrounded by a group of attractive women as he says, "I don't always drink beer, but when I do, I prefer Dos Equis. Stay thirsty, my friends."[11]

The most interesting man's story continues to evolve. What the brand refers to as "legend lines" continue to build the character's mystique. Here are just a few:

- His charm is so contagious vaccines have been created for it.
- The police often question him just because they find him interesting.
- His personality is so magnetic he is unable to carry credit cards.
- He's a lover, not a fighter. But he's also a fighter, so don't get any ideas.
- He can speak French, in Russian.
- His mother has a tattoo that reads "Son."

Dos Equis actively engages its audience with good humor and a twist: the most interesting man in the world isn't a typical, hard-sell pitchman for the product. He seems a somewhat reluctant product endorser when he says, "I don't always drink beer..."

So who is this mysterious character who seems to actually *believe* that he is the most interesting man in the world? Veteran actor Jonathan Goldsmith brings the character to life. He says, "He hangs out with pygmies. He's a teacher. He's a sage. He's a shaman. He's a fantasy. He's an illusion of things past."[12] Senior brand manager Paul Smailes says that, "more than anything else, [drinkers] really wanted to be seen as interesting by their friends."[13] The brand went against the grain to create a world-traveling, bigger-than-life, rogue of a character who wouldn't be seen as a threat to a much younger target market. The brand's research showed that it might be effective to create someone the customer could aspire to become. Kheri Tillman, VP of marketing for Dos Equis, said, "What's interesting about him is that he doesn't compete with our consumer. He's more of an inspiration. He's an aspirational target for them."[14]

The magic of breaking the rules has worked wonders for the brand. In 2009 the ad campaign went national, and Dos Equis continues to break sales records each year, outpacing all other imports. The brand has become the sixth-best-selling import beer, with over $74 million in sales.[15] "Dos Equis is an awesome brand," said Anthony Bucalo, an analyst at Banco Santander SA. "It's not limited to hipsters in Vermont drinking microbrews, or blue-collar workers drinking Bud."[16]

Until the Dos Equis campaign struck gold, it had been tough sledding for import brands to break through to an audience dominated by domestic beer advertising. Consider that in 2008 there were 261 beer brands advertising on TV in the United States. "There's never really been an import brand that's been built so clearly through advertising," said Benj Steinman, publisher of *Beer Marketer's Insights*.[17]

Dos Equis has engaged its customers by concentrating on one primary social channel, Facebook. The page doesn't take itself too seriously: "Created in Mexico by a German brewmaster, formulated in the 19th century to welcome the 20th, XX is simultaneously a mysterious dichotomy and a world-class beer brand."[18] The Facebook page has nearly two million followers, and people constantly submit their own legend lines for consideration.

The brand is extending its most interesting attitude with the formation of the Most Interesting Academy. The mission is to "inform, inspire, and equip" fans to lead more extraordinary lives. The company has created the Stay Thirsty Grant competition, where fans can apply to live out their fantasies, "whether it's base jumping in Bangkok, preparing rattlesnake soup for royalty, or traversing the Amazon."[19]

Imagine if your brand openly embraced the Customer CEO rebellion that's in everyone by having more fun with its products and promotions. Dos Equis found it could be quite contagious and profitable.

Gaming to Please

There are a lot of places to go hang out to watch a game. The thing is, the food's not very good, but what do you expect?
Gary, Houston, Texas
Participant in a customer interview about sports bars

On a cold December night, there was a rowdy gathering at the Green Dragon Tavern on Union Street in the north end of Boston. While beer no doubt helped fuel the patrons' passions, there wasn't the usual trash talking about sports so common in places like the Green Dragon. There weren't any flat-screen televisions showing a Celtics or Patriots game that night. And there was more serious business to discuss. The year was 1773, and that group of men, called the Sons of Liberty, decided it was a fine place to start a revolution. The American Revolution. Little did the men who gathered that night realize that the pursuit of happiness they were fighting for would result in sports bars in the twenty-first century. In America, it seems there's always been a little rebel in all of us.

Buffalo Wild Wings Grill and Bar (BWW) is a nearly eight-hundred-restaurant national chain that doubled in size in less than seven years. *Forbes* magazine ranked it as one of its top-ten fastest-growing retailers in 2011.[20] BWW knew that its core sports-obsessed male customers wanted a place of rebellion.

They wanted more than just some beer and food and a place to hang out and watch sporting events. Through market research, the company determined that its customers were fun, edgy, high-energy, yet also easygoing. They wanted a complete sports fan experience.

So that's what the restaurant resolved to give them. BWW decided to bring the experience of a pregame tailgate party inside. That's how the idea of tablegating, "a party at every table," was born. The chain created a unique atmosphere that replicated the one you might find at a pregame party in a stadium parking lot. It's a fun and social environment designed to build interaction between customers and staff. There are usually ten projection screens and another fifty high-definition flat-screen monitors in each location. In a typical year, sixteen thousand sporting events are shown live.[21] That's a lot of sports to watch.

To build excitement and new sales, BWW enlisted SCVNGR, a social gaming application, to create competitive games right in the stores. Customers downloaded a special challenge app onto their mobile devices, and BWW created a series of customer contests that awarded prizes to winners. One example was a March Madness challenge. In three months, 184,000 customers registered to play. "It's very social—almost like tailgating, but in a restaurant," said Christopher Mahl, senior vice president of brands at SCVNGR. "Each customer came in about 2.4 times in the last two months," he said of the SCVNGR users. "That's more frequent than our other guests who may come in five or six times a year."[22] BWW also created an interactive website to support the idea of tablegating, which attracts over 1.5 million unique visitors a month. Its Facebook page has more than 4.75 million fans. By being rebellious, Buffalo Wild Wings has become a $2 billion enterprise.[23]

There's opportunity for every company to put tools in customers' hands that help them easily promote the brand. But remember that customers want to participate in something that is interesting or exciting for them, not simply promotional for you.

Blowing and Growing

As a marketing manager for an industrial shipping company, it's like pulling teeth to get my bosses to ever approve doing anything different or the least bit controversial. They are so afraid of offending somebody. It's kind of like the military: just name, rank, and serial number. So everybody's brand is just the same. It's boring.

Donna, Charlotte, North Carolina
Participant in a focus group about business-to-business marketing

Carey Smith is known as "Chief Big Ass." The longtime entrepreneur wears the label with a tremendous amount of pride. He worked in a variety of business pursuits before finally hitting on the idea that would help put him on the map. Smith decided to enter the business of blowing hot air. Literally.

Farmers in the dairy business know that cows quit eating when they get hot. Hot cows don't produce milk. A noisy fan cools a cow off but causes stress to the cow, so the result is still no milk. The solution was to mount extremely large and quiet fans overhead, cooling all the cows in the barn without stress. The steady breeze created by these large fans cools surrounding areas between eight and sixteen degrees fahrenheit. Cooler cows meant more milk and happier dairy farmers. This was the initial problem that Smith and his team were tasked to solve. The company was originally called HVLS (High Velocity/Low Speed). Fortunately for Smith, that name didn't resonate with very many people.

What did grab customers' attention was the huge size of the fans the company was building. These giant fans can be as large as twenty-four feet in diameter. Upon first seeing an HVLS fan, many prospects apparently exclaimed, "That's a big-ass fan!" I first saw one of the company's fans while I was touring a client's manufacturing facility, and my reaction was the same. It's one of those perfect descriptions that comes along only so often. Smith knew he was on to something so he commissioned a complete rebranding of the company, including using a cartoon donkey as a logo. Big Ass Fans is a company known as a rebellious, independent, and innovative place to work. Smith said that Blue Grass Airport, near the company's headquarters in Lexington, Kentucky, wouldn't sell the company ad space because of its controversial name. There are fewer complaints now than there were in the early days, in 2008, when the name was changed. "It's amazing how little flak we get for it anymore," Smith said.[24]

Big Ass is a company that connects with its customers. Procter & Gamble veteran Al Barlow, the company's chief marketing officer, said, "Obviously, P&G has always done a very good job of listening to its customer, and that's something anyone could learn and apply. You need to understand what their unmet needs are, and the way to do that is to talk to them, incessantly. And that's what we do, and I've pushed that here at Big Ass Fans."[25]

One of the ways the company differentiates itself from its competition is by foregoing the traditional model of selling through distributors and retailers. Instead, Big Ass Fans employs a sixty-five-person sales team that deals directly with every customer. The company has given away well over 300,000 Big Ass hats featuring its Fanny the Donkey logo. It refuses to publish a price list on the website, saying that every customer deserves a custom solution to his problem because every cooling condition and space is unique. And Big Ass Fans come with a ten-year warranty because of the fans' advanced design. Smith believes so strongly in discovering innovation that he plows 8 percent or more of the firm's revenues into research and development. "That's what makes this company unique. They're just looking at fans and then innovating on those fans and coming up with new technology," said Justin Molavi, an industry analyst for market researcher IBISWorld.[26]

The next frontier for Big Ass? It's called Haiku, the company's first foray into the residential market. "It makes no noise, moves beaucoups of air and uses very, very little energy," Smith said.

Ever the rebel, Smith wants complete independence and says he will reject all potential suitors who want to acquire the company. "We don't need somebody else telling us what to do. We can do whatever the hell we want."[27]

Profiting from the Power of Rebellion

Tapping into the Power of Rebellion will take your company to a very different place. There is enormous opportunity because so many of your competitors are simply afraid of rebellion. Look at the clear competitive advantage André Rieu, Dos Equis Beer, Buffalo Wild Wings, and Big Ass Fans have over their competitors. How difficult do you think it would be for anyone to catch up to them? As you have seen, these companies have employed much more than clever brand positioning, although that's clearly important. Each of these maverick enterprises is meeting people at an important place by letting them have fun and breaking the bonds of normal commerce.

The great professional hockey player Wayne Gretsky once said, "I skate to where the puck is going to be, not where it has been." These business leaders recognized that anyone could perform a regular concert, brew a beer, open a restaurant, or sell a commodity like a fan. But not everyone can envision a better future by unlocking powerful demand built around the idea of breaking a few rules. Can you really imagine:

- a symphony orchestra performance where people dance or stand in their seats, swaying to the music?
- a young person's beer built on the shoulders of an old guy who defies everything boring or ordinary?
- a bar and grill breaking sales records by bringing a rowdy sports crowd inside to play computer games?
- a boring industrial manufacturer that has turned an entire industry upside down by stating the obvious (that's a big-ass fan!)?

You profit from the Power of Rebellion by having the courage to harness an undeniable competitive advantage. Actually, it's a decisive competitive advantage. There are really only two choices when you consider the Power of Rebellion as a potential way to set yourself apart.

You Can Choose to Be Boring

You can tread the path that's accepted and completely inoffensive. That's okay. Most companies fit into this box and communicate bland information about themselves, what I like to call FFL (facts, figures, and legacy, as in, "John Smith founded our company in 1936"). I can tell you that customers don't care because not only is it irrelevant to them, it is boring. If you are in a competitive market, your customers will eventually have other choices and you will see a slow but steady erosion of your business. You can count on it.

You Can Choose to Be Bold

The bold path is different and rebellious. Some will absolutely love you, while others will refuse to return your phone calls. But you will be long remembered. Take along the people who want to go on an adventure. In today's marketplace, customers hunger for companies that have a sense of humor and irony.

If you have rules, rewrite them. Ask what customers hate about your company and listen closely. Don't be offended and defensive. When customers open up—and they will—shut up and listen. In your marketing, appeal to the person your customer aspires to be. Be the kind of company he wants to have a beer with. That's the Power of Rebellion in action.

(How well does your organization engage the Power of Rebellion? Visit customerceopowercheck.com to download our free diagnostic tool.)

11

The Power of Purpose

Key Customer CEO Question:

Do we share the same values?

Imagine if you turned on your television one night to see a commercial featuring an attractive young woman speaking directly to the camera. In a sincere, heartfelt manner she had a simple message for you:

> Isn't it time that a company told you the truth? Well, here it is: we don't care what you think. We're here to sell you stuff you don't really need. The more of it, the better. Our products don't really do what we say they will do and we won't service them when they break. And that warranty we sold you? C'mon, you've got to be kidding! Our job is

to simply try to separate you from as much of your money as humanly possible. Please don't be offended. It's not personal, it's just business as usual. We're just doing our job of enriching ourselves at your expense. The only world we want to improve is our own. Now, can we please have your credit card number?

The Power of Purpose is the last and the most difficult Customer CEO power. I've left it for last because it is the toughest stuff in this book. In this chapter, I am confronting something that every business leader needs to consider. It doesn't matter whether you are a CEO, a middle manager, or a frontline employee. You are a leader in your own way because you have influence for good or bad. This influence extends to both your coworkers and your customers. Take a moment to reflect on whether the ad I just described is a message that your company is subliminally sending customers and prospects. I'm not talking about just the advertising you do. That's just the tip of the iceberg. It's what is— or isn't—underneath that counts. It's your values.

Right up front, let me confess that I am a dyed-in-the-wool, free-enterprise-loving capitalist. I believe that in most cases, the best road to prosperity for people and nations is through free-market capitalism. A company's first order of business must be to make a profit. In fact, it should strive to maximize its profit. Profit provides the necessary capital to innovate, retain the best talent, and sustain the enterprise. But the question is, are too many of us failing to lead enterprises with core values that we can share with our customers and employees?

John Mackey, CEO of Whole Foods, said, "Long-term profits are maximized by not making them the primary goal."[1] This is so true. When I began my sales and marketing career in the 1970s, I observed that some of the other salespeople and managers were engaged in some kind of strange Kabuki dance each month in order to maximize their commissions. This often meant bending the rules, including what was called "hanging paper." This was the unethical practice of writing orders that the customer had never authorized, hoping the invoice would somehow slip by an unsuspecting accounts payable person. I watched it happen. These kinds of games never made sense to me. I felt that if I could just focus on generating better results for my customers the commissions would take care of themselves. And they did.

A high calling for us as businesspeople is service. But a higher calling than service is *character*. In my customer research work over the years, I have seen a growing hunger on the part of customers for companies that don't just talk a good game, but really live by a more virtuous code. I have heard the phrase "just do the right thing" more times than I can count. I believe that the poor attitude we so often see exhibited by employees is a direct result of poor values leadership. And here's the deal: If company leadership tolerates poor values by allowing customers to be treated poorly, why should we expect customers to behave any better?

Let's be frank: for many companies facing the complexities of modern business, it is too much work to create, teach, and live values. We'd rather cut corners and look the other way. Human resource departments are so worried about lawsuits that disciplining employees is often a thing of the past. Poor values are tolerated. So, many customer-facing employees are left in their jobs far too long. To the customer, service becomes a bad joke. The public relations and advertising spewing forth from these brands hardly resemble the reality the customer encounters on a daily basis.

Customers, no matter how cynical they may appear, are hungry for a difference. They want the truth. Entrepreneur and philanthropist John Paul DeJoria said, "The world today needs truth and we're not getting enough of it…speak the truth, don't be afraid of it. People need to know the truth of what's going on… just take responsibility and you move on."[2]

Simon Mainwaring founded We First, a social brand consultancy, because of the disconnect he saw between business as usual and what people want. He believes there is a new set of dynamics in today's marketplace, with two integrated forces at work. First, customers want a better world and second, the future of profit is purpose. He says:

> As more consumers insist that capitalism work in the service of a better world, companies will become increasingly purposeful, and thus more profitable. Replacing the old capitalism paradigm of supply and demand, this dynamic between profit and purpose will become the new economic principle that drives the marketplace. Consumers who want a better world will drive the profits of corporations that provide greater purpose through their activities. Meanwhile, corporations that provide too little purpose for consumers will fail.[3]

Another way of seeing this is to understand that more and more of your customers today buy the why before the what. They want to do business with companies they can believe in. You have to be crystal clear in defining your purpose. Spell it out as plainly and as often as possible. Customers have dreams and hopes, and they want to align themselves with yours.

Clarity around values also speaks volumes to your employees. Tony Hsieh, CEO of Zappos said, "A funny thing happened when we actually communicated [our purpose] to our employees. We found that suddenly employees were a lot more passionate about the company, a lot more engaged, and when customers called they could sense the personality at the other end of the phone wasn't there just for a paycheck."[4] When a jury in the infamous patent case found that Samsung had unfairly competed against Apple, Apple CEO Tim Cook sent an e-mail to his employees that said, in part, "For us this lawsuit has always been about something much more important than patents or money. It's about values. We value originality and innovation and pour our lives into making the best products on earth. And we do this to delight our customers, not for competitors to flagrantly copy."[5]

When high-profile CEOs are saying that the values of their companies outweigh money, something new is beginning to stir in the marketplace. It gets back to what we believe in most deeply. The John Huston classic movie *The Treasure of the Sierra Madre* tells the story of three Americans who ended up in Tampico, Mexico, in search of fortune. A crusty old-timer named Howard, played by the fine character actor Walter Huston, tells his two younger partners, Dobbs and Curtin, played by Humphrey Bogart and Tim Holt, that a desire for gold will eventually destroy any man who spends a lifetime in search of it: "As long as there's no find, the noble brotherhood will last, but when the piles of gold begin to grow, that's when the trouble starts...I've never known a prospector who died rich. That's what gold does to a man's soul...men are friends until they find the gold."

In the final scene of the movie, a windstorm gathers up the gold dust the men have extracted from the mountain and blows it all away. All of their efforts have been in vain. Howard bursts into a manic fit of laughter. With tears rolling down his cheek, he exclaims, "This is a great joke played on us by the lord, fate, nature, or whatever you prefer. But, who or whatever played it had a sense of humor. The gold has gone back to where we found it."[6]

And that's really everyone's story, isn't it? In the end, the gold goes back to where we found it. This creates an added imperative for our organizations to build themselves on a foundation of rock-solid values like integrity, fairness, and honesty. The world has experienced far too many Ponzi, Enron, WorldCom, and Madoff schemes. Your business, in fact every business, can be a force for good. There are big problems in the world that our political system has failed to solve. Business can begin to shoulder a greater role in being the solution, not the problem. Instead of being portrayed as the guys in black hats, how about reversing the trend?

It starts now with the Power of Purpose. Your customers are demanding nothing less, so you might as well get started. Let's take a look at three companies that already have.

One for One for Everyone

When you hear the offer, "Buy one, get one free," you think about taking two things home in your shopping bag, whether you need it or not. I never even considered the idea of buy one, and send the other to someone who needs it more than me. That's absolutely brilliant!

Andi, Orlando, Florida
Participant in a customer interview about retail

Have you ever thought of your business as something more like a movement? If you haven't, you aren't alone. Most of us are so fixated on keeping our trains running on time that we don't stop to consider making a bigger mark on the world. Neither did Blake Mycoskie.

In 2006 he was in Argentina, and the last thing on his mind was starting a new business, much less a movement. Mycoskie said, "When I went down to Argentina the idea was to play polo, drink some red wine, have some fun, clear my mind."[7] He noticed that the polo fields were adjacent to some of the poorest areas of Buenos Aires. He was shocked at the abject poverty he saw. That's when he realized the children had no shoes. Local shoe drives only collected people's castoffs and worn-out shoes. They were falling apart and weren't suitable for children. Mycoskie saw a dire need and believed he could do something about it. He asked, "What if I started a shoe company and every time I sold a pair of shoes, I gave a pair away?" That was how TOMS began. The brand is built on a simple promise: "With every pair you purchase, TOMS will give a pair of new shoes to a child in need. One for One."[8]

The lack of shoes actually creates three major problems for people. The first is health. The World Health Organization says that 740 million people are affected by hookworm, a soil-transmitted parasite that can cause serious illness.[9] According to

UNICEF, nearly ten million children under the age of five die every year from largely preventable causes.[10] The Asian Development Bank estimates that thirty thousand people living without shoes in just a single Philippines landfill walk over debris that includes syringes and glass.[11]

The second problem is education. In many areas of the world, governments require children to wear shoes in order to attend school. The third is individual opportunity. Healthy children are much more likely to be successful students and future citizens who can play a role in building better communities. TOMS has given away over one million pairs of shoes (as of 2012) in twenty-five countries. The company conceived a new way to create awareness for this cause with an event called One Day Without Shoes. Over 250,000 people, including business executives, agree to go shoeless. This annual event has been enlisting new people in the mission since 2007.[12]

Part of the TOMS model is to hand deliver the shoes to children. Employees and volunteers place each pair on a child's feet. Mycoskie believes that meeting a child one on one intimately connects each employee with her purpose. Seeing the joy of a child, Mycoskie says, "That changes your life."

The One for One idea has taken root around the world. There are now dozens of like-minded "philanthropic entrepreneurs" with similar business models for a wide array of products, including books, baby clothing, toys, socks, T-shirts, health food, vitamins, pet beds, cold-weather clothing, and toothbrushes. In 2011, TOMS launched its second product line. TOMS Eyewear provides prescription glasses or eye surgery for children.

The Power of Purpose is really about giving customers a way to spend their money with companies that care to make a difference. Blake Mycoskie simply saw a need and he filled it. He encourages everyone in business to do the same: "Don't wait for perfect timing. Don't think that you've got to be in this perfect place. Just do it."[13]

Discover the Statue Inside

I have learned the hard way that low price only takes you so far. Price is important, but I want suppliers with character. If a company treats their employees badly, how in the world will they treat me as customer? I look for people who will do the right thing; those are the ones I can count on.

Sam, Pittsburgh, Pennsylvania
Participant in an interview, general contractor

The dictionary defines the word "luck" as "the force that seems to operate for good or ill in a person's life, or simply 'good fortune.'" Charles Luck III says luck has nothing to do with his company's success. He's the chairman of Luck Companies. Luck says, "Our success is based on people, not necessarily on machines. My dad taught me that if you treat people fairly, then they'll treat you the same."[14] A simple quarry that started in 1923 has been continuously operated by the same family for nine decades. The company has firmly held to the same simple values. With more than a thousand employees, the Richmond, Virginia-based company operates more than fifteen plants in two states. The Luck Companies run a diversified enterprise, producing construction aggregates, architectural stone, and clay tennis courts and accessories. They also operate a real estate development company.

"We've never lost our focus on people, yet at the same time we provide products and services that our customers can depend on," explains president and CEO Charles Luck IV. "We've taken our core product, a rock, and wrapped it with services and features that are unique in our industry. And we remain committed to our customers, neighbors, associates, and communities to never lose sight of our roots, and the core values my grandfather established more than 85 years ago."[15]

But a crisis driven by rapid growth caused the company to consider a different, somewhat unorthodox path. The management team began pulling in different directions and the company was losing touch with its customers' needs. It decided to enlist a leadership development firm, Holt Development Services (an outgrowth of Holt Cat, discussed in chapter 7). Holt had experienced a similar situation in the late 1980s, and it led the company to adopt a values-based leadership (VBL) model of operating. Harry M. Jansen Kraemer Jr., author of *From Values to Action: The Four Principles of Values-Based Leadership*, explains the underlying idea behind VBL: "When you truly know yourself and what you stand for, it is much easier to know what to do in any situation. It always comes down to doing the right thing and doing the best you can."[16]

With the company a firm believer in VBL, Luck is out to change people by helping change business. "We are incredibly passionate about this," Luck said. "Our mission as a company is to ignite the potential in people around the world so they can positively impact others using values-based leadership."[17] After serving as a senior executive for the company for more than twenty years, Mark Fernandes is now an ambassador of sorts, with a mission to help companies adopt VBL. The Luck website boldly asks:

What's your purpose? Transforming your organization by identifying and adhering to a powerful mission provides purpose for your employees and customers. They understand where your company is going and why it exists. Your mission gives clarity for decision-making, long-term strategic planning and communication. Your company and associates have a clear purpose to align around, work toward and get passionate about. Values Based Organizations develop a mission that leads with making a difference in the world, ultimately resulting in a strong business performance.[18]

The company believes that people can only truly reach their potential when the things they hold dear—their values—align with those of the customers they serve and the organizations they work for. Not content to just print the sentiment on posters to hang in their break rooms, the Luck Companies have created a philosophy it calls "Ignite Human Potential." Here's how the Luck website explains this concept:

> Know who you are, where you are and what's going on around you. Awareness is knowing who you are, recognizing how you are feeling and what you are thinking… awareness involves recognizing your strengths, your weaknesses and your stumbling blocks and looking inward to see if you are showing up the way you really want to. When you are aware of and act in alignment with your core values, your effectiveness in influencing and impacting those around you increases dramatically.[19]

Luck teaches that there's no one right way to implement values-based leadership. It encourages businesses of every size to spend time studying some of the hundreds of models that exist. The company explains that VBL cannot work without the "training, process alignment, accountability, stories, and rituals and celebrating success" being in place.

Italian artist and engineer Michelangelo said, "Every block of stone has a statue inside it, and it is the task of the sculptor to discover it." Luck has proven that every company can discover how to embrace the Power of Purpose by chipping away at the stone to find the values hidden within.

Don't Buy Our Stuff

It seems to me that everyone is so busy buying and selling stuff that no one takes the time to consider what we are really doing anymore. I mean, how many more things do I really need?

Kendrick, Austin, Texas
Participant in a customer interview about corporate responsibility

Imagine visiting a car showroom and being told by a salesperson, "Thanks for coming by, but we aren't selling any cars today." How about driving by an electronics store that had a huge sign in its entrance announcing, "No gadgets for sale today." Or a mall that locked its doors and had loudspeakers blaring, "Please return home. There's nothing for sale here, so move along." What about clicking on your favorite e-commerce site only to find a black screen with a scrolling message that said, "Cyberspace is closed. Return to your planet." At the very least, you would be irate because, as a customer, you would be mightily inconvenienced by these attitudes of indifference. You'd think, "What kind of nerve do these people have?" It's your right to buy things whenever and wherever you want!

Patagonia, the outdoor clothing and gear company, took such a pause in 2011 on the two biggest shopping days of the year, Black Friday and Cyber Monday. Visitors to Patagonia's website were greeted with a large screen announcing "Don't Buy This Jacket." Subscribers to the company's online newsletter were e-mailed the same. The company had also taken out full-page ads in national newspapers that read:

> The environmental cost of everything we make is astonishing. Consider the R2 Jacket [shown in the ad], one of our best sellers. To make it required 135 liters of water, enough to meet the daily needs (three glasses a day) of 45 people. Its journey from its origin as 60% recycled polyester to our Reno warehouse generated nearly 20 pounds of carbon dioxide, 24 times the weight of the finished product. This jacket left behind, on its way to Reno, two-thirds its weight in waste. And this is a 60% recycled polyester jacket, knit and sewn to a high standard; it is exceptionally durable, so you won't have to replace it as often. And when it comes to the end of its useful life we'll take it back to recycle into a product of equal value. But, as is true of all things we can make and you can buy, this jacket comes with an environmental cost higher than its price."[20]

The ad concluded with a radical statement: "Don't buy what you don't need. Think twice before you buy anything."

Consider for a moment that more than 70 percent of the U.S. economy is driven by consumer spending. We have to sell a lot of SUVs, flat-screen TVs, and powder blue ski jackets to keep the ball rolling. Patagonia is a for-profit business that depends on that spending to continue. Was this some kind of clever "anti-marketing" marketing ploy designed to drive sales despite the company's altruistic admissions? Perhaps, but Patagonia was going where very few companies have ever gone before.

People who were shocked by the anti-jacket campaign didn't really know Patagonia. The company was publicly embracing the Power of Purpose by shouting out its own set of values. It didn't matter if anyone agreed. Patagonia is a company that has always marched to the beat of a different drummer, and this was the direction founder and sole owner Yvon Chouinard had been headed for a long time. He never wanted to get big just for the sake of getting big. In 2004, he wrote, "At Patagonia, we are dedicated to abundance. We don't want to grow larger, but want to remain lean and quick. We want to make the best clothes and make them so they will last a long, long time. Our idea is to make the best product so you can consume less and consume better."[21]

Harvard Business School professor Forest Reinhardt says Patagonia is a one-of-a-kind business: "I've never seen a company tell customers to buy less of its product. It's a fascinating initiative. Yvon has the confidence to pull it off."[22] Chouinard values something more than making the next sale. "I never even wanted to be in business," he says. "But I hang onto Patagonia because it's my resource to do something good. It's a way to demonstrate that corporations can lead examined lives."[23] In *Let My People Go Surfing*, his 2005 autobiography, he wrote, "If I had to be a businessman, I was going to do it on my own terms."[24]

In 1991, financial problems and high debt nearly sank Patagonia. The crisis caused Chouinard to reassess everything. He decided that the things he valued the most would guide every corporate decision going forward. The company began to look at everything through the prism of sustainability. Every product was redesigned using more environmentally friendly materials. He created a policy of taking full responsibility for the company's products. Customers could ask Patagonia to replace, resell, or recycle, and it would. And, as unlikely as it seems, Chouinard has formed a strategic alliance with Walmart to help the much larger business understand that green business practices are really good business. He realizes that he has a rare opportunity to impact American business in a big way by being true to his own values. He said he always thought the revolution would bubble up from below, but now says, "It's starting at the top."[25]

Profiting from the Power of Purpose

Your potential and existing customers are searching for companies they can believe in. They are bombarded with thousands of messages and touch points every day promising purpose, but they are rarely getting it. Cynicism is born from insincerity and dishonesty. What do you expect? You will profit by embracing the Power of Purpose and transforming your culture. It doesn't matter what size you are or what industry you are in. Look at the amazing impact TOMS Shoes, Luck Companies, and Patagonia are having; their ability to transform people's lives is inspirational. Your customers and employees want to become united with a company that says what it believes and then proceeds to live it.

Purpose Must Be Real, Not Imagined

Every company will face moments of definition, no matter how established it is. Whether driven by growth (Luck), financial calamity (Patagonia), or identity (TOMS), storms will come. It's as inevitable as the business cycle. But why wait for a crisis to find your true inner core? It's hard work. You have to be willing to ask yourself and your people what you really believe in. Do you want to change things at your company? If so, what do you want to change? And don't kid yourself. This is not some jargon-ridden theoretical exercise. It is personal. If you aren't willing to examine yourself, you are wasting your time. Transformation can only happen if it starts at the top. Be willing to give yourself and your team the time to really work on this. Rome wasn't built in a day, and neither is purpose.

Purpose Must Live in the Now

As we saw with the Power of the Platform, today everything happens in real time. If you fail at purpose, it will be broadcast far and wide. You cannot control it so you have to live it all the time. And when you fail at it you have to make serious amends quickly or you risk losing everything you have built: your reputation and your enterprise. This is why it is so critical to teach purpose, so it can permeate the entire organization. For example, imagine how Patagonia's "Don't Buy This Jacket" campaign would have failed if the entire organization wasn't onboard on those crucial Christmas shopping days. Your company must always be moving forward and projecting your purpose for the world to see.

Purpose Cannot Just Hang on the Wall

There are a lot of companies that profess to be values based. They like to memorialize their values on posters that hang on walls at headquarters and branch offices. They have entire sections of their websites describing them. While there's nothing wrong with visual reminders, the real question is whether those values are there for show or whether they are being lived across the enterprise, top to bottom. Honestly, in many companies, the values statements have become invisible. I know employees and customers who advocate "ripping them off the wall" if the company cannot properly align itself with its values. Sometimes the unwritten message from leadership is "Do as we say, not as we do." Your company's purpose shouldn't be subject to the blowing winds of management change. The best Customer CEO companies realize that continuity of values is what customers value most. They don't really care who's at the helm; they care about the way they are being treated.

Purpose Must Be Overcommunicated

Inside and outside, every day and in every way, you must lead by extolling your purpose. Truly, I believe it is one of the single most important jobs because so many others aspects of the business flow from it. But here's the thing: purpose isn't just a set of statements, it is a strategic advantage. You must embed it into the DNA of the organization. Every employee is a reflection of the company's values. You cannot talk about values too much. We learn and understand through repetition. In your company you should talk to new recruits about what they can expect in terms of your purpose. Train new people on your values. Every leader at every level should model those values. Recognize employees publicly who show a commitment to your purpose.

Purpose is serving. Service is more than a set of performances, it is an attitude and a deeply held belief of the heart.

(How well does your organization engage the Power of Purpose? Visit customerceopowercheck.com to download our free diagnostic tool.)

12

The Customer Thinking Solution

Why are you like
everybody else?

As Apple was beginning its reboot in 1997 with the return of Steve Jobs as CEO, the company decided to send a direct message to customers and competitors that it was becoming a different kind of company. The "Think Different" campaign showed us glimpses of the "misfits" we celebrate, from Albert Einstein to Muhammad Ali to Pablo Picasso. Actor Richard Dreyfuss brought the poetic copy to life with a matter-of-fact yet inspirational voice-over narration:

Here's to the crazy ones.

The misfits. The rebels. The troublemakers.

The round pegs in the square holes. The ones who see things differently.

They're not fond of rules. And they have no respect for the status quo.

You can quote them, disagree with them, glorify or vilify them. About the only thing you can't do is ignore them. Because they change things.

They push the human race forward. While some may see them as the crazy ones, we see genius.

Because the people who are crazy enough to think they can change the world, are the ones who do.[1]

Apple laid down the gauntlet to the world to say it was back. "Think Different" was much, much more than an ad campaign; it was a rallying cry for a company ready to declare that it was back and that it was different. I believe that if you embrace the powers of the Customer CEO you will be different too.

And Now for Something Completely Different

Now that you have looked at the nine powers of the Customer CEO, it's time to consider what to do about what you've learned. I am going to ask you to consider these powers, but perhaps not in the way you imagine. For a few minutes, I want you to open your business minds to something completely different.

For far too long, marketing people at many companies have marketed with blinders on. Decisions are often made with imprecise and incomplete information. Many marketing executives look at things primarily from a right brain perspective; all art, little science. This is because many of them lack basic quantitative and analytical skills, and thus, they are reluctant to be held accountable. Far too often, they answer hard-nosed marketing ROI questions from the C-suite with soft answers like, "Our advertising is designed to increase our brand awareness." Change starts with being willing to be educated about how marketing expenditures really affect financial performance. For example, if you don't know who the most profitable customers are, how can you justify spending targets for your limited resources on the non-profitable ones? Marketing must be efficient to be effective in a world of diminishing resources. It's failing if it is not held to that standard. Marketing must measure what's really important. In short, if you can't measure it, you shouldn't spend it.

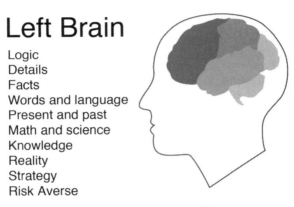

Left Brain

Logic
Details
Facts
Words and language
Present and past
Math and science
Knowledge
Reality
Strategy
Risk Averse

Figure 12–1: Grow a Left Brain

The tools are available to measure marketing results, so there's no longer any excuse. Now you can optimize your media spending and even attribute customer conversion to both online and offline sources. This is no time for staying stuck in the past. Simply put, more professional marketers need to grow a left brain.

On the other hand, more non-marketing executives across the enterprise, whatever their function, need to grow a right brain. Using creativity is a better way to compete going forward. The future is the fusion of the two. Author Dan Pink, in his book, *A Whole New Mind*, wrote, "Our left brains have made us rich. Powered by armies of Drucker's knowledge workers, the information economy has produced a standard of living that would have been unfathomable in our grandparents' youth. Their lives were defined by scarcity. Ours are shaped by abundance."[2]

Pink makes a persuasive case for the re-unification of both sides of our brains. Yes, our analytical, number-crunching, strategy-loving, left brains have taken business further than most could ever have imagined. But, the secret to our continued growth and prosperity lies in the merger and acquisition of the creative, metaphor-filled, music-loving right brains we have so often been taught to ignore. According to Pink:

> To flourish in this age, we'll need to supplement our well-developed high tech abilities with aptitudes that are "high concept" and "high touch." High concept involves the ability to create artistic and emotional beauty, to detect patterns and opportunities, to craft a satisfying narrative, and to come up with inventions the world didn't know it was missing. High touch involves the capacity to empathize, to understand the subtleties of human interaction, to find joy in one's self and to elicit it in others, and to stretch beyond the quotidian in pursuit of purpose and meaning.[3]

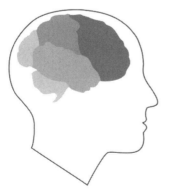

Right Brain

Feelings
Big Picture
Imagination
Symbols and images
Present and future
Philosophy
Beliefs
Fantasy
Possibilities
Risk taking

Figure 12–2: Grow a Right Brain

High concept, high touch is a long way from the nitty-gritty world of business operations, corporate finance, and human resources. These are the fundamentals taught in business school that allow us to function. Let me be clear: mastery of these functions is mandatory in business; without them, you will perish. But I believe the future calls us to be something different and better. I want you to be able to tear down the walls between the two sides of your brain.

The Customer Thinking Solution

Your company can start profiting with the approach I call "Customer Thinking." Customer Thinking balances the analytical and the intuitive. It allows every business to fuse its left-sided quantitative customer intelligence (big-data analytics) and its right-sided qualitative customer insight (empathy) into a single, integrated framework.

When you put together the analytical and the intuitive you are, in essence, marrying the "what" with the "why." Too many companies rely exclusively on data to explain the what. Ironically, many have so much data that they can't process it and make it meaningful. But the quantitative is only one piece of the puzzle. The "why" is the missing link for becoming a Customer CEO company. The purpose of Customer Thinking is twofold: to increase customer engagement and to improve the customer experience. If you accomplish those two things, you will build a thriving, differentiated brand and maximize the lifetime value of your customers.

Design Is Our Model

People often aren't sure where to begin the process of change or how to do it. It should be clear by now that every business must become customer-centric if it hopes to survive. Customers have so many choices today that any company that thinks it is indestructible is kidding itself. There are no permanently great industries or companies anymore. This means enterprises must shift from a "What can we sell them?" to a "What job do they need to get done that we can help them with?" mentality. They must quit thinking about how much money they can get from customers and start thinking about what values customers truly want to pay for.

This new Customer Thinking discipline requires a shift away from traditional market research. Most companies dedicate the majority of their budgets to market studies and surveys from third parties. I propose you consider dedicating resources to a much more intimate approach to the customer. Apply the same methodologies product designers use to create deeper engagement and better experiences. The Customer Thinking Solution begins with an honest evaluation of how you deliver the nine powers of the Customer CEO.

Start with the Customer CEO Power Check

I have created a simple set of tools I call the Customer CEO Power Check. This exercise serves as an audit of how your company scores across the nine Customer CEO powers. You will be asked key questions about your performance across a ten-point continuum. After scoring each power, you'll plot the results on a Customer CEO Power map, and any gaps will become clear. This tool will serve as a framework for your company before you launch any new customer insight initiative. The Power Check is absolutely free, and you can download it at customerceopowercheck .com for your use.

New Ways to Understand Your Customers

I believe that IDEO, the world-famous design and innovation consultancy, provides a strong model to emulate. IDEO believes that breakthrough ideas come when companies immerse themselves in the lives and environments of their customers. The company practices a relatively new kind of customer research, most commonly referred to as empathic design. Empathic design offers you an up-close way to observe real people as they lead their lives. Empathic design is about discovering latent customer needs that the customers themselves may not be able to articulate. For example, the average businessperson may not have been able to describe an iPad and its many uses before Apple created it. But a careful observer who noted the pain of lugging a five- to seven-pound laptop through airport security would have seen a potential market for a lightweight tablet computer. People's lives could be improved with a new device that eliminated the excess weight and hassle. Empathic research taps into latent rather than explicit needs.

Another method design firms like IDEO use is ethnography; it's another way to understand culture through observation. An *ethnography*, as the term is used in marketing, is a graphical representation of the culture of any group of people. Using low-cost video and photography, it's an additional way to capture how people are experiencing your products. Researchers gather visual and written evidence to bring back to share with executives. The Hyundai Santa Fe example we discussed is a good example of how ethnography helps companies embrace emerging trends they might not uncover back at the office. By visiting model homes in the neighborhoods of their "Glamour Moms," the researchers were able to note the warm wood and color palettes that appealed to these women. Hyundai designers applied these insights to the interior design of the new Santa Fe.

Contextual interviewing is another design approach to understanding the customer that is gaining popularity in product innovation circles. This type of customer interview has been refined by Dr. Richard "Dick" Lee, CEO of Value Innovations, Inc. Contextual interviewing is a process intended to uncover the unmet, unarticulated needs of customers. Lee explained that companies of all sizes are seeing exceptional results by breaking the rules of traditional market research. Lee says:

Conventional wisdom is that you have to interview a large number of people to be statistically correct. But our client companies are finding that's not the case at all. Our rule of thumb is to stop the interviews when we aren't hearing anything new. Amazingly, that can happen with as few as six interviews. Also, our approach is to interview two people at once. Rather than an interview, it is really a discussion. The key to the best outcome is providing a visual framework to the customer to keep the interview moving forward. We do that with value curves that clearly illustrate the subject matter. Contextual interviewing really works if the interviewer is prepared and keeps the interview tightly focused.[4]

Lee uses three rounds of interviews in his Value Innovation projects, describing these rounds as, "Listening, shaping, and defining."

With these emerging techniques, many people are quick to dismiss the traditional focus group. However, I believe the death of the focus group has been greatly exaggerated. I continue to find that well-targeted groups provide strong baseline information if they are well structured and facilitated. These panels can be extremely effective in measuring perceptions and understanding behavior. I adapted an advertising technique called benefit testing to create shorter, less expensive, and more "focused" focus groups. Using storyboards similar to those used in film and television commercial concept development, we are able to have the panel review and rank a large number of business ideas without wasting time on irrelevant information.

In recent years, we have begun to use what I call the "club" model. In this format, customer groups are recruited to meet over much longer periods of time, in some cases up to a year. These become essentially self-directed, customer-led groups in which the participants become friends. Company researchers are present in the room, not hidden behind the mirror munching on M&Ms, like in a typical focus group room. These customer clubs are great ways to test new ideas and spot emerging trends. Procter & Gamble also uses these types of groups in their Consumer Village R&D facility in Cincinnati, Ohio.

Another new technique is the customer journey map. These maps lay out every step customers take to acquire a product or service. For example, if a fan wished to attend an André Rieu concert, a customer journey map would look at the pre-purchase, purchase, and post-purchase periods to understand her expectations, experiences, and satisfaction/dissatisfaction with the event. Insight might lead to improved pre-concert information about seat locations and transportation. Social media has also added a new element to the journey because it offers that critical understanding of what people are saying during and after the event.

Telling the Stories

It's important to bring Customer Thinking to life inside your company with short videos that tell your customer stories. Think of these as internal commercials. They are intended to inform and teach your colleagues, and to create empathy in them for your customers. Make Customer Thinking come alive by clearly showing the strengths and weaknesses of your offerings, as well as the opportunities.

An Ongoing Process

Customer Thinking is not a one-time event. You must continue to stay connected to your customers and prospects, with what I call "pulsing." Your doctor takes your pulse every time you visit her; you must do the same when it comes to customer understanding. That is, you must continue to refine your insight over time by interacting with your customers regularly. We live in a dynamic marketplace and you must stay in constant touch with the customer. It's important to provide easy ways to listen and engage. Use your website as a master listening post to capture customer conversations, comments, and critiques. Your site also offers an important way to facilitate engagement. Look for ways to gain real-time product and service feedback.

Profit + 11

Customer Thinking will enhance satisfaction, increase engagement, and improve the experience for the Customer CEO. The obvious profit will come through top- and bottom-line growth and increased market share. But the big payoff is that, through the Customer Thinking solution, you will profit in eleven other critical areas of business performance, which will drive your company further ahead than it has ever been. If you get Customer Thinking right, you will experience what I call "Profit + 11."

Figure 12–3: Profit + 11

1. **Unorthodox inspiration.** Customer Thinking will supercharge the flow of great ideas. This goes both ways between company and customer. You will hear your customers' ideas and can test your own ideas on them. Ultimately, this can inspire everyone in your sphere, employees and customers alike.

2. **Intense passion.** Imagine a time in the future when you can spark deeper passion for your company from your customers and employees. Customer Thinking will light this fire.

3. **Unmovable trust.** Break through the door of cynicism by building a deep, abiding trust between your customers and your company. Don't think it's possible? Go back and read some of the stories in this book about companies that are doing it.

4. **Fanatical loyalty.** Strive to become a brand that is a cult. It doesn't matter what industry you are in, how long you've been in business, or your size. Fanatical customers are your best brand ambassadors; if you let them, they will sell a lot of your goods and services by shouting your goodness from the rooftops.

5. **Creative cost reduction.** This is one of the greatest hidden gems to come from building deeper customer relationships. Customers will literally tell you, and show you, how to make more money by eliminating features and services that offer no value to them.

6. **Trendsetting innovation.** Great companies know that they don't have a monopoly on great ideas. Tap into your customer's brains and experiences. Give them an incentive to partner with you to deliver innovation. Remember, it doesn't have to be the next great, earth-shattering thing; innovation is really incremental improvement of what already is.

7. **"Best-in-class" brand awareness.** It's easy to forget in today's overheated marketing world that your customers sell you through "word of mouth" every single day. Social media has simply amplified their voices. This is why a brand can become a sensation almost overnight if it strikes the right chords with its customers.

8. **Compelling culture transformation.** Every company needs to be shaken up, no matter how good it is. Why? Because no one can ever know enough. Lose the arrogance and be humble enough to let your customers help you transform the culture. Every employee has something important to learn about the value of serving others as a vocation.

9. **Dramatic growth.** Here's the secret: if you just master one or two of the nine Customer CEO powers, you will hit a home run in terms of profitable, sustainable growth. Become champions of all nine and your business will not only change forever, it will surge past all competitors. Why settle for business as usual any longer?

10. **Intriguing storytelling.** Stories are the universal way we learn from each other. Business schools teach through case studies, yet in the practice of business, we tend to rely on our own experiences and opinions as the final word. We often ignore the stories that count the most, those of our customers. Customer stories are the Trojan horse of future success. When you learn and master the stories of your customers, you will be able to communicate with and persuade stakeholders in a fresh, new way. Telling the stories of your customers will keep the spotlight on them, where it belongs.

11. **Dominant competitive advantage.** A Customer CEO company is light-years ahead of ordinary competitors. If you think about just a few of the companies we have discussed in this book, it is easy to see why they blow their competitors away.

If you have customers, Customer Thinking is the best way to keep your customer plate spinning at peak performance. The result of this simple yet highly effective approach can be a better multinational corporation, tire store, insurance agency, heavy equipment dealership, or local dry cleaning service. It doesn't matter. When you adopt this approach, you really will profit from the power of your customers.

There's an old saying that a rut is nothing more than a grave with the ends knocked out of it. In this hypercompetitive time, you cannot afford to get stuck in a rut; it is death. Customer Thinking will help you become a Customer CEO company. You will go from not understanding the market to leading it. Customer CEO companies achieve lasting results. And that's the whole point, isn't it?

13

Becoming the Customer CEO Champion

Key Customer CEO Question:

What are you waiting for?

After thirty-five years on the front lines of business, I have been asked many times by young entrepreneurs what I believe is the most important element for success in business. I used to say knowing how to sell. Peter Drucker said our primary purpose in business is to create new customers every day. I believe that. But after a few years of riding the roller coaster of crazy business cycles, I began saying that knowing how to mitigate risk was the most important thing. If you take too many risks, the odds will catch up with you no matter how smart you might be. On the other hand, if you fail to take enough risks, and you refuse to change, you're a sitting duck.

Now that I look back on it, I was wrong about selling and risk. While both are critical to your success, the most important factor is truly caring about your customers. There's a Chinese proverb that says, "A man without a smiling face must not open a shop." It's your job as a leader to define what success looks like to customers right up front. If you miss the mark on that, everything else is pointless. You won't make the sale, market the product, deliver the experience, or grow your business. It was only after I seriously began to think about the writing of this book that the name Customer CEO formed in my mind. To me, it was the perfect metaphor for everything I have believed and practiced in my career.

People who are serious about understanding and serving their customers will lead the next generation of great companies. We have looked at a few of them in this book, like Ingvar Kamprad of Ikea, who built his business on the idea that what was good for the customer was good for the company. Jeff Bezos of Amazon said his customer, "is the most important person in the world." The late Rich Snyder of In-N-Out Burger believed that servant-based leadership was a calling. Music entrepreneur André Rieu said he wanted to give classical music back to the people. And, of course, Blake Mycoskie of TOMS said giving away shoes changes the lives of both the receiver and the giver.

Business is much more than getting to scale, having the best intellectual property, or finding cutting-edge innovations. Your business's legacy will ultimately be built on the human touch. And this must start at the top. Effective leadership requires a deep empathy for and embrace of the customer. If those who lead don't believe, how can you expect anyone else in the organization to deliver? Customer service, engagement, and experience aren't just idle words. They are the proof of your commitment.

Adopt the Customer CEO Manifesto As Your Own

I invite you to join me on a mission to understand, cultivate, and nurture customers across every nook and cranny of your enterprise. Feel free to adopt the Customer CEO manifesto as your own.

The greatest asset companies possess is not their building, reputation, or heritage. It's their customers.

This is even truer in today's social business marketplace. Customers now share or control the conversation with brands, the distribution of their marketing, and, ultimately, their sales.

To some companies, this is a threat. To the smartest, it's an opportunity.

Customer power has unlocked the potential of co-creation marketing, innovation, and distribution. It has transformed every employee into a valuable listening post. It provides leaders with myriad channels through which they can humanize their brands.

The success stories of the future will be those companies that partner with their customers, that lead with listening, inspire their employees through purpose, and bring their core values to life in ways that are meaningful to customers and employees alike.

The Customer CEO philosophy provides the road map for such success by relieving customer frustration, exposing the futility of fad strategies, and empowering companies to leverage these timeless business fundamentals for success in today's marketplace: brand integrity, employee participation, and customer engagement.

Your Journey Starts Now

Once you decide to understand the Customer CEO, you should strive to become the Customer CEO Champion. This simply means you need to become the in-house leader and advocate for the customer. Don't get me wrong; this doesn't mean cutting prices or agreeing with whatever whim or complaint a customer might have on a particular day. It's much bigger than that. It's philosophical. Either you believe that embracing the customer is the right thing to do or you don't. You can agree that a customer-centric enterprise is better for your long-term success or you can disagree. But if you agree, then you must become a champion.

- **A Customer CEO Champion understands it's all about customers.** You communicate internally and externally from the customer's point of view. You learn to tell customers' stories ahead of your own. This points your entire organization in a better way. Instead of being focused on your products, speak about how your products change people's lives.
- **A Customer CEO Champion continuously creates value for customers.** You recognize that value is much more than price and that customers want to do business with a company that truly desires to offer them great value at a fair price. Added value can take many forms, including product features and services offered. But, never forget that the greatest way to add value is by enhancing the experience.
- **A Customer CEO Champion celebrates customers at every possible opportunity.** Customer CEOs do this by loving and believing in their customers. This will inspire the company to look for new and exciting ways to transform the culture into a Customer CEO culture. Employees will begin to recognize opportunities to serve where they have missed them before.
- **A Customer CEO Champion is on the constant search to deliver higher performance for the customer.** Helping customers do the important jobs they are already trying to do better should become your company's calling card.
- **A Customer CEO Champion is simple.** Look to remove complexity at every opportunity. It will make both customers

and employees happier. Commit to fewer steps, less fine print, and a no-hassle way of doing business.

- **A Customer CEO Champion loves to say yes.** Learning to first say yes instead of no is essential. Make yes the first word to come out of an employee's mouth. Be obsessed with serving.
- **A Customer CEO Champion provides a platform for two-way conversations with customers.** Good or bad, you aren't afraid to hear what your customers have to say. That's the best way to figure out what to fix. Remember, someone, somewhere, is already listening to your customers and will eventually figure out how to steal them from you if you aren't listening.
- **A Customer CEO Champion enjoys breaking the rules.** Customer CEO Champions understand that it's perfectly all right to have fun. There is no better engagement strategy for customers and employees than letting go of the reins and enjoying the ride together.
- **A Customer CEO Champion has the opportunity to be about a bigger purpose than just doing business.** These companies can use their influence to change the world.

As the Customer CEO Champion, you want to help your people make the customer experience richer and easier. Start to enjoy customer interaction instead of dreading it. A Customer CEO Champion gives his team permission to connect. By encouraging more interaction on a daily basis, you motivate everyone to become more invested in making a difference.

In closing, the great leaders I have had the privilege of knowing have a special bond with both their customers and their employees. These people transcend business as usual. These leaders constantly seek new ways to close the gaps that separate them from their customers. Some of it is just talking. But that's the point. A mutually valuable relationship is much deeper than money. Time spent getting to know people is an investment in your future. It's no less important than research and development, operations or logistics. It's no secret that it is a lot cheaper to keep an existing customer than acquire a new one. Actually, if you become a Customer CEO Champion, you will do both. Strive to become a true servant leader by spreading these ideas. This is how you will best profit from the power of your customers. The effect of this book can be so powerful that everyone in your company will be transformed into a Customer CEO Champion too. So share it.

America's first venture capitalist, Georges F. Doriot, put it well when he said, "Without action, the world would still be an idea." Take the first step to become the Customer CEO Champion. You'll be glad you did. In serving others first, you will serve yourself.

EPILOGUE

Dear company,

I'm not sure what got your attention, but you've changed. I can tell by the way you have begun to treat me. Lately, I can tell you are paying attention to the little things. It's like you've been listening to my friends and me as we've been talking to each other. You rolled back those latest price hikes, and that surprised us. A little money goes a long way these days, so we appreciate it.

But we've also noticed a different tone. When I called with a billing question yesterday, the person I spoke with actually seemed to care. He wasn't rushed and we had a real conversation. He agreed that I had a good point and he corrected it in my favor on the spot! He not only said yes, I think he actually broke the rules. I've already told my Facebook friends about it because it was so...well, unexpected.

If you are willing to listen to my point of view, maybe there's a good reason for me to stick around. Oh, the customer service rep also asked if I had heard about your new program to support our local kids with after-school music lessons. Thanks for being their champion. He said that you were looking for volunteers, so I'm going to check that out. I told him it was a great idea but he said that one of your customers suggested it. So if you are open to suggestions, I've got some great ideas, too.

Let's talk.

Sincerely,
The Customer CEO

NOTES

The customer comments throughout this book are based on surveys, focus groups and interviews my firm has conducted. Much
of the other material is based on my own business experience.

Chapter 1

1. Reed Hastings, "In Wyoming...," Reed Hastings' Facebook
page, September 20, 2011, http://www.facebook.com/reed1960/posts/
10150304609004584.

2. Lauren Effron, "Netflix CEO Reed Hastings Says Company Has
'Sincere Regret' Over Handling of Service Changes," ABC News, September 26, 2011, accessed September 03, 2012, http://abcnews.go.com/
Business/netflix-ceo-reed-hastings-company-sincere-regret-customers/
story?id=14608865.

3. "Henry Ford, Faster Horses and Market Research," *Research Arts*,
January 25, 2011, http://www.researcharts.com/2011/01/henry-ford-faster
-horses-and-market-research/.

4. Bo Burlingham and George Gendron, "The Entrepreneur of the
Decade," Inc.com, accessed September 03, 2012, http://www.inc.com/
magazine/19890401/5602.html.

5. Garsen O'Toole, "My Customers Would Have Asked for a Faster
Horse," *Quote Investigator*, July 28, 2011, http://quoteinvestigator.com/2011/
07/28/ford-faster-horse/.

6. Ian Sherr, "Apple's Secrets Revealed at Trial," *Wall Street Journal*,
August 5, 2012, www.wsj.com. http://online.wsj.com/article/SB1000087239
6390443687504577567421840745452.html

7. John Seabrook, "How to Make It," *New Yorker*, September 20, 2010,
66-73.

8. Don Peppers and Martha Rogers, Ph.D., *Rules to Break and Laws to
Follow*, (New York: John Wiley, 2008) 24.

9. David F. Wallace, "2005 Kenyon College Commencement Address" (speech given at commencement, Kenyon College, Gambier, Ohio), May 25, 2005.

Chapter 2

1. "Sam Walton," Entrepreneur.com, October 9, 2008, http://www.entrepreneur.com/article/197560.

2. Noah Plaue, "How the Average American Has Changed Since the 1960s," *Business Insider*, July 7, 2012, http://www.businessinsider.com/how-the-average-american-has-changed-since-the-1960s-2012-7?op=1.

3. Jeanne Sahadi, "Why Nearly Half of Us Don't Pay Income Tax," CNNMoney, April 26, 2012, http://money.cnn.com/2012/04/26/pf/taxes/income-tax/index.htm?hpt=hp_c1.

4. "57% Say Housing Prices Will Take More Than Another Three Years to Recover" *Rasmussen Reports*, June 19, 2012, http://www.rasmussenreports.com/public_content/business/general_business/june_2012/57_say_housing_prices_will_take_more_than_another_three_years_to_recover.

5. Kristen Purcell, Joanna Brenner, and Lee Rainie. *Search Engine Use 2012* (report), March 9, 2012, http://pewinternet.org/~/media/Files/Reports/2012/PIP_Search_Engine_Use_2012.pdf.

6. *The Virtuous Circle: The Role of Search and Social Media in the Purchase Pathway* (report), February 2011, http://www.wpp.com/NR/rdonlyres/CA49ED29-06A4-4E10-A1F0-C25BAA35CF2A/0/groupm_search_the_virtuous_circle_feb11.pdf.

7. *15th Annual Global CEO Survey* (report), 2012, http://www.pwc.com/gx/en/ceo-survey/pdf/15th-global-pwc-ceo-survey.pdf.

8. *2011 R&D/Innovation and Product Development Priorities Survey* (report), 2011, http://www.growthconsulting.frost.com/web/images.nsf/0/05621478A97C323C862579E40007729B/$File/2011GlobalR&%20InnovationSurveyReport.pdf.

9. *2012 Global CEO Study* (report), IBM, 2012, http://www-935.ibm.com/services/us/en/c-suite/ceostudy2012/.

10. http://dictionary.reference.com/browse/generation+Y.

11. John Zogby, "The CENGA Generation and 2012," *John Zogby* (blog), June 18, 2012, http://thejohnzogby.com/index.html.

12. http://dictionary.reference.com/browse/millennial+generation.

13. Adrian Kingsley-Hughes. "600,000 Apps in Apple's App Store, Yet I Can't Find Anything I Want," ZDNet, April 6, 2012, http://www.zdnet.com/blog/hardware/600000-apps-in-apples-app-store-yet-i-cant-find-anything-i-want/19549.

14. Clayton M.Christensen, Scott D. Anthony, and Erik A. Roth, *Seeing What's Next: Using the Theories of Innovation to Predict Industry Change* (Boston: Harvard Business School Press, 2004), 101.

15. Machiavelli, Niccolò, Quentin Skinner, and Russell Price. *Machiavelli: The Prince* (Cambridge: Cambridge University Press, 1988), http://www.constitution.org/mac/prince06.htm

Chapter 3

1. Kevin V. Johnson, "Chronicles Got *Everything Started.*" *USA* Today, May 14, 1998.

2. Brian Lowry, " 'Seinfeld,' a Cinderella Story That Went From Fable to Legend," *Los Angeles Times*, April 2, 2001, http://articles.latimes.com/2001/apr/02/entertainment/ca-45737.

3. Larry David, "The Couch," *Seinfeld*, NBC, October 27, 1994.

4. "About IKEA," Our Business Idea, http://www.ikea.com/ms/en_GB/about_ikea/the_ikea_way/our_business_idea/index.html.

5. "IKEA Statistics," Statistic Brain, May 26, 2012, http://www.statisticbrain.com/ikea-statistics/.

6. John Simmons, "IKEA—Brand of the Many," *The Guardian*, June 12, 2005, guardian.co.uk.

7. Pandora Internet Radio, accessed July 2012, http://www.pandora.com/.

8. Laura Green, "How Tim Westergren Dials in Approval from Pandora's Customers and Employees to Drive Growth," Smart Business, February 1, 2012, http://www.sbnonline.com/2012/02/how-tim-westergren-dials-in-approval-from-pandora%E2%80%99s-customers-and-employees-to-drive-growth/.

9. Snapshots, "Tim Westergren: Future of Pandora Radio," Tim Westergren: Pandora Interview, accessed July 2012, http://www.snapshotsfoundation.com/tim-westegren-pandora-interview.

10. Ibid.

11. Mike Gathright, "Leadership Perspective: Obsess Over Customers," *Baylor Business Review*, March 29, 2012, http://bbr.baylor.edu/obsess-over-customers/.

12. George Anders, "Inside Amazon's Idea Machine: How Bezos Decodes the Customer," *Forbes*, April 04, 2012, http://www.forbes.com/sites/georgeanders/2012/04/04/inside-amazon/.

13. "Amazon 2012 Annual Report," Amazon.com, 2012, http://phx.corporate-ir.net/phoenix.zhtml?c=97664&p=irol-reportsannual.

14. "Amazon Media Room," Amazon.com, accessed September 10, 2012, http://phx.corporate-ir.net/phoenix.zhtml?c=176060&p=irol-factSheet.

15. Anders, "Inside Amazon's Idea Machine."

195

16. Brad Tuttle, "Apple, L.L.Bean—and Especially, Amazon—Score Big in Online Shopping Satisfaction," TIME.com, May 14, 2012, http:// moneyland.time.com/2012/05/14/apple-l-l-bean-and-especially-amazon -score-big-in-online-shopping-satisfaction/.

17. Barney Jopson, "Amazon 'robo-pricing' Sparks Fears," *Financial Times*, July 8, 2012, http://www.ft.com/intl/cms/s/0/26c5bb7a-c12f-11e1 -8179-00144feabdc0.html.

18. Kevin Freiberg and Jackie Freiberg, *Nuts!: Southwest Airlines' Crazy Recipe for Business and Personal Success* (New York: Broadway Books, 1998), 250.

19. Stuart Elliott, "A Spate of Ads Gives Vent to That Howard Beale Feeling," *The New York Times*, June 26, 2008, http://www.nytimes .com/2008/06/26/business/media/26adco.html?pagewanted=print.

20. Freiberg and Freiberg, *Nuts!*

21. *2011 Edelman Trust Barometer* (report), 2011, http://trust.edelman .com/.

Chapter 4

1. David Lee Roth, *Crazy from the Heat* (London: Ebury, 2000), 12.

2. Tim Donnelly, "How to Sell on Value Rather than Price," Inc .com., July 20, 2011, http://www.inc.com/guides/201107/how-to-sell-on -value-rather-than-price.html.

3. Penn Jillette, and Teller, "The Truth about Bottled Water," Penn & Teller: *Bullshit!*, July 3, 2007.

4. W. Chan Kim and Renée Mauborgne, *Blue Ocean Strategy: How to Create Uncontested Market Space and Make the Competition Irrelevant* (Boston, MA: Harvard Business School Press, 2005), 120–25.

5. Bob Greene, "Will 'Showrooming' Kill Businesses," CNN.com, June 17, 2012, http://www.cnn.com/2012/06/17/opinion/greene-showrooming/ index.html.

6. Ann Zimmerman, "Can Retailers Halt Showrooming," *Wall Street Journal*, April 11, 2012, www.wsj.com. http://online.wsj.com/article/SB100 0142405270230458770457733437067 0243032.html.

7. Aaron Smith, *The Rise of In-Store Mobile Commerce* (report), January 30, 2012, http://pewinternet.org/Reports/2012/In-store-mobile-com merce.aspx.

8. George Anderson, "Nordstrom Delivers with Free In-Store Shipping," RetailWire.com, March 13, 2012, http://www.retailwire.com/discussion/ 15873/nordstrom-delivers-with-free-in-store-shipping.

9. Marisa Taylor, "Target Tried to Fight Off Online Retailers," NBC News, January 24, 2012, http://bottomline.nbcnews.com/_news/2012/01/ 24/10226938-target-tries-to-fight-off-online-retailers?lite.

10. Warren Buffet, *2008 Berkshire Hathaway Investor Letter*, 2008, http://www.berkshirehathaway.com/letters/2008ltr.pdf.

11. Becky Quick, "Car Salesmen: Still Sexist, Still Stupid," CNNMoney, February 28, 2012, http://finance.fortune.cnn.com/2012/02/28/sexist-car -salesmen/.

12. Ibid.

13. "Hyundai's Value Touted as Rival Car Dealers Seek Models." *Las Vegas Review-Journal*, June 1, 2012, http://www.lvrj.com/drive/hyundai-s -value-touted-as-rival-car-dealers-seek-models-156216465.html.

14. Hannah Elliott, "Year of the Hyundai," *Forbes*, June 23, 2009, http:// www.forbes.com/2009/06/23/hyundai-automobiles-krafcik-business -autos-hyundai.html.

15. Heather Kluter and Doug Mottram, "Touch the Market," *PDMA Visions*, June 2007, 15–19.

16. Ibid

17. Hyundai Motor America corporate website, accessed September 10, 2012, http://www.HyundaiUSA.com/assurance.

18. Melanie Warner, "How Hyundai Is Gaining Market Share," CBSNews, June 05, 2009, http:// www.cbsnews.com/8301-505125_162 -51309290/how-hyundai-is-gaining-market-share/.

19. Landon Wood, telephone interview with author, July 5, 2012.

20. Lab Armor corporate website, www.labarmor.com.

21. Steven Greenhouse, "How Costco Became the Anti-Walmart," *The New York Times*, July 17, 2005, http://www.nytimes.com/2005/07/17/ business/yourmoney/17costco.html?pagewanted=all.

22. Michael Beyman, "No-Frills Retail Revolutions Leads to Costco Wholesale Shopping Craze," CNBC, April 25, 2012, http://www.cnbc .com/id/47177291/No_Frills_Retail_Revolution_Leads_to_Costco_Whole sale_Shopping_Craze.

23. Greenhouse, "How Costco Became the Anti-Walmart."

24. "Ryanair Stewardess Falls from Aircraft," *I Hate Ryanair* (blog), May 8, 2012, http://www.ihateryanair.org/ryanair-stewardess-falls-from-aircraft/.

25. "Hostess Plummets from Ryanair Plane in Sweden," *The Local*, May 8, 2012, http://www.thelocal.se/40712/20120508/.

26. Ryan Air corporate website, accessed May 8, 2012, http://www .ryanair.com/en/terms-and-conditions. Sarah Lyall, "No Apologies From the Boss of a No-Frills Airline," *The New York Times*, August 1, 2009, http://www.nytimes.com/2009/08/01/world/europe/01oleary.html? pagewanted=all.

27. Ray Massey, "Ryanair to Sell Standing Room Only Tickets for £4. Funded by Charging Passengers to Use the Toilet," *Daily Mail*, July 1, 2012, http://www.dailymail.co.uk/news/article-1291103/Ryanair-sell-standing -room-tickets-4–funded-charging-passengers-use-toilet.html.

28. David P. Brown, "Standing Seats Are NOT Coming to a Ryanair Plane Near You," *Airline Reporter*, July 6, 2012, http://www.airlinereporter .com/2010/07/standing-seats-are-not-coming-to-a-plane-near-you/.

Chapter 5

1. "Criteria for Performance Excellence," National Institute of Standards and Technology, February 17, 2010, http://www.nist.gov/baldrige/ publications/criteria.cfm.

3. Oliver Burkeman, "Happiness is a glass half empty," http://www .guardian.co.uk/lifeandstyle/2012/jun/15/happiness-is-being-a-loser -burkeman Dina Bass, "Microsoft Is Said to Stop Releasing New Models of the Zune," Bloomberg, March 14, 2011, http://www.bloomberg.com/ news/2011-03-14/microsoft-said-to-stop-releasing-new-zune-models-as -demand-ebbs.html.

4. Ji Hoon Jhang, Susan Jung Grant, and Margaret C. Campbell, "Get It? Got It. Good! Enhancing New Product Acceptance by Facilitating Resolution of Extreme Incongruity," University of Colorado Leeds Business School, October 2012, http://leeds.colorado.edu/asset/publication/extre meincongruity.pdf.

5. Damien Scott, "The 50 Worst Fails in Tech History," Complex. com, April 29, 2011, http://www.complex.com/tech/2011/04/the-50-worst -fails-in-tech-history/digiscents-ismell.

6. William Buxton, *Sketching User Experience: Getting the Design Right and the Right Design* (San Francisco, CA: Morgan Kaufmann, 2007), 9.

7. Ibid.

8. John T. Gourville, "Eagle Sellers and Stony Buyers: Understanding the Psychology of New-Product Adoption," *Harvard Business Review* 11, no. 6 (June 2006): 99–106.

9. Janet Pogue, "Tear Down This Wall," *Employee Benefit News*, March 1, 2009, http://ebn.benefitnews.com/news/tear-down-wall-2670421-1 .html.

10. "Apple Stores Have Seventeen Times Better Performance Than the Average Retailer," Asymco company website, April 18, 2012, http:// www.asymco.com/2012/04/18/apple-stores-have-seventeen-times-better -performance-than-the-average-retailer/.

11. Allen Adamson, "Ron Johnson on Lessons Learned from Apple About Gaining an Edge As a Retail Brand," *Forbes*, July 19, 2012, http:// www.forbes.com/sites/allenadamson/2012/07/19/ron-johnson-on-lessons -learned-from-apple-about-gaining-an-edge-as-a-retail-brand/.

12. "Apple Stores Have Seventeen Times Better Performance Than the Average Retailer," Asymco company website.

13. David Morgenstern, "Recalling a Summer When Steve Jobs Saved Apple and the Mac," ZDNet, October 6, 2011, http://www.zdnet.com/blog/apple/recalling-a-summer-when-steve-jobs-saved-apple-and-the-mac/11318.

14. Horace Dediu, "How Much Does an Apple Store Cost?" Asymco company website, October 14, 2011, http://www.asymco.com/2011/10/14/how-much-does-an-apple-store-cost/.

15. "Construction Cost Estimating," *Reed Construction Data*, accessed May 5, 2012, http://www.reedconstructiondata.com/rsmeans/models/retail-store/.

16. Carl Sewell and Paul B. Brown, *Customers for Life: How to Turn That Onetime Buyer into a Lifetime Customer* (New York: Doubleday, 2002), 141.

17. Zeke MacCormack, "Wait Is over for Fans of Buc-ee's, Its Restrooms," *San Antonio Express-News*, May 8, 2012, http://www.mysanantonio.com/default/article/Wait-is-over-for-fans-of-Buc-ee-s-its-restrooms-3540830.php.

18. Katie McFadden, "Best Western Using High-Tech Cleaning Techniques," *Travelers Today*, March 30, 2012, http://www.travelerstoday.com/articles/1824/20120530/best-western-using-high-tech-cleaning-techniques-best-western-hotels-blacklight-uv-light-csi-clean-d.htm.

19. Barbara DeLollis, "CSI Hotel Room: Best Western Goes High-tech to Clean," Usatoday.com, May 31, 2012, http://travel.usatoday.com/hotels/story/2012-05-30/CSI-hotel-room-Best-Western-goes-high-tech-to-clean/55270430/1.

20. Tim Carmody, "Expressing Technology: A Roundtable with Sir James Dyson," Wired.com, September 17, 2011, http://www.wired.com/business/2011/09/james-dyson-roundtable/all/.

21. John Seabrook, "How to Make It," *New Yorker*, September 20, 2010, 66–73.

22. Beth Carney, "Dyson's Magic Carpet Ride," *Businessweek*, March 31, 2005, http://www.businessweek.com/printer/articles/231780-dyson-s-magic-carpet-ride?type=old_article.

23. Susie Mesure, "James Dyson: He Sweeps As He Cleans As He Spins. What's Next from the Ideas Factory?" *The Independent*, May 27, 2006, http://www.independent.co.uk/news/business/analysis-and-features/james-dyson-he-sweeps-as-he-cleans-as-he-spins-whats-next-from-the-ideas-factory-479931.html.

24. Bill Breen, "The Business of Design," *Fast Company*, April 1, 2005. http://www.fastcompany.com/55581/business-design.

25. Robert Brunner and Stewart Emery, *Do You Matter?: How Great Design Will Make People Love Your Company* (Upper Saddle River, NJ: FT Press, 2009), 46.

Chapter 6

1. Tim Engle, "Ex-Trader Joe's Employee Writes a Mostly Complimentary Tell-All," *The Kansas City Star*, June 30, 2012, http://www.kansascity.com/2012/06/29/3683333/trading-tales-of-trader-joes.html.

2. Beth Kowitt, "Inside Trader Joe's," *Fortune*, September 6, 2010, 86–92.

3. Barry Schwartz, *The Paradox of Choice: Why More Is Less* (New York: Ecco, 2004), 9–12.

4. "The Tyranny of Choice: You Choose," *The Economist*, December 16, 2010, http://www.economist.com/node/17723028.

5. Kowitt, "Inside Trader Joe's."

6. Christopher Palmeri, "Trader Joe's Recipe for Success," *Businessweek*, February 20, 2008, http://www.businessweek.com/stories/2008-02-20/trader-joes-recipe-for-success.

7. Jena McGregor, "Leading Listener: Trader Joe's," *Fast Company*, October 1, 2004, http://www.fastcompany.com/51637/leading-listener-trader-joes.

8. Gitte Larsen, "Why Megatrends Matter," Copenhagen Institute for Future Studies, May 2006, http://www.cifs.dk/scripts/artikel.asp?id=1469.

9. "Our Foundations," Jyske Bank corporate website, accessed April 15, 2012, http://dok.jyskebank.dk/Unit/jyskebank/jyskebankinfo/Ourfoundations/.

10. "This Danish Branch Is Beyond Cool," *The Financial Brand*, October 29, 2008, http://thefinancialbrand.com/2893/jyske-bank-branch/.

11. Dana Mattioli, "Lululemon's Secret Sauce," *The Wall Street Journal*, March 22, 2012, http://online.wsj.com/article/SB10001424052702303812904577295882632723066.html.

12. "Looking Good in Tights and Unafraid to Be Rich and Powerful," *The Gazette*, Canada.com, August 12, 2008, http://www.canada.com/montrealgazette/news/arts/story.html?id=b8781702-3cba-49a5-88f0-7f7c77c71b3c.

13. Mattioli, "Lululemon's Secret Sauce."

Chapter 7

1. Charles Mingus, interview, *Mainliner Magazine*, July 1977.

2. Henry Petroski, *Invention by Design: How Engineers Get from Thought to Thing* (Cambridge, MA: Harvard University Press, 1996) 78–79.

3. Tom Kelley and Jonathan Littman, *The Art of Innovation: Lessons in Creativity from IDEO, America's Leading Design Firm* (New York: Currency/Doubleday, 2000), 28.

4. Matthew E. May, *In Pursuit of Elegance: Why the Best Ideas Have Something Missing* (New York: Broadway Books, 2009), 12.

5. Patrick Spenner and Karen Freeman, "To Keep Your Customers, Keep It Simple," *Harvard Business Review*, May 2012, http://hbr.org/2012/05/to-keep-your-customers-keep-it-simple/ar/1.

6. "The 2012 NRN Top 200," *Nation's Restaurant News*, June 25, 2012, http://nrn.com/nrn-top-100.

7. In-N-Out Burger corporate website, In-n-out.com, accessed September 10, 2012.

8. Stacy Perman, *In-N-Out Burger: A Behind the Counter Look at The Fast-Food Chain that Breaks All the Rules* (New York, NY: Collins Business, 2010), 7.

9. Perman, *In-N-Out Burger*, 139.

10. Dan Macsai, "The Sizzling Secrets of In-N-Out Burger: Q&A With Stacy Perman," *Fast Company*, April 23, 2009, http://www.fastcompany.com/1273180/sizzling-secrets-n-out-burger-qa-stacy-perman.

11. Blake W. Gray, "The Story behind the Story That Made Wine History," *SFGate*, June 16, 2005, http://www.sfgate.com/wine/article/The-story-behind-the-story-that-made-wine-history-2662065.php.

12. W. Chan Kim and Renée Mauborgne, *Blue Ocean Strategy: How to Create Uncontested Market Space and Make the Competition Irrelevant* (Boston, MA: Harvard Business School Press, 2005), 31–35.

13. "Orders Are Stacking Up," *The Paul Merage School of Business Dean's Quarterly*, Spring 2012, http://merage.uci.edu/deans-quarterly/spring2012/stacking.html.

14. Conor Friedersdorf, "A New Way to Drink Wine: Trading in the Bottle for the Four-Pack Stack," *The Atlantic*, April 2012, http://www.theatlantic.com/business/print/2012/04/a-new-way-to-drink-wine-trading-in-the-bottle-for-the-four-pack-stack/255486/.

15. "Dr Oz: Stacked Wines, Mastrad Apple Cooker & Magisso Cake Server," *Dr. Oz Fans* (blog), April 18, 2012, http://www.drozfans.com/dr-oz-diet/dr-oz-stacked-wines-mastrad-apple-cooker-magisso-cake-server/.

16. MP Dunleavy, "Did 'Sex and the City' Ruin You Too'" *MSN Money*, June 20, 2012, http://money.ca.msn.com/savings-debt/mp-dunleavey/article.aspx?cp-documentid=24595560.

17. "Shoe Stores," Hoovers, accessed April 14, 2012, http://www.hoovers.com/industry/shoe-stores/1520-1.html.

18. *Global Footwear Manufacturing Report*, IBISWorld, 2010, http://www.just-style.com/store/samples/2010_IBISWorld%20Global%20Style%20Sample%20Industry%20Report.pdf.

19. Rob Merlino, "Onesole Dominique Barteet Interview," *Shark Tank Blog*, June 7, 2012, http://sharktankblog.com/3064/onesole-dominique-barteet-interview.

Chapter 8

1. Stanley Marcus, *Quest for the Best* (New York: Viking Press, 1979), 44.
2. Ibid.
3. *Miracle on 34th Street*, film, directed by George Seaton, 20th Century Fox, 1947, DVD.
4. David K. Randall, "Only the Store Is Gone," *The New York Times*, February 19, 2006, http://www.nytimes.com/2006/02/19/nyregion/thecity/19gimb.html.
5. Jan Carlzon, "What Business Leaders Can Learn From 'Moments of Truth': An Interview With Former SAS CEO Jan Carlzon," interview by Bob Thompson, *Customer Think*, January 11, 2006, http://www.customerthink.com/interview/jan_carlzon_moments_of_truth.
6. Robyn C., "Discount Tire, Austin, TX," review on Yelp, March 31, 2012, www.yelp.com/biz/discount-tire-austin-3.
7. Max Jarman, "After 50 Years, Service Still Drives Discount Tires," *AZ Central*, January 2, 2011, http://www.azcentral.com/business/articles/2011/01/02/20110102good-service-still-drives-Discount-Tires-0102.html.
8. Jarman, "After 50 Years, Service Still Drives Discount Tires."
9. *Tire Industry 'Legends'* Publication no. 35167310, 13th ed. Vol. 26, *Tire Business*, 2008.
10. Ibid.
11. Michael Rosenbaum, "The Synergy Mirage: A Case Study," *Chief Executive*, February 17, 2012, http://chiefexecutive.net/the-synergy-mirage-a-case-study.
12. "Our 'raison D'être,'" Chateauform' company website, accessed December 12, 2011, http://www.chateauform.com/en/the-home-of-seminar/the-concept/5.
13. Ibid.
14. Marion Debruyne, "The Devil Is in the Detail: Learnings on How to Be a Customer-Focused Organization by Chateauform," *Marketing Blog Vlerick*, July 23, 2012, http://marketingblog.vlerick.com/2012/07/23/research/the-devil-is-in-the-detail-learnings-on-how-to-be-a-customer-focused-organization-by-chateauform/.
15. "Benjamin Holt," Invent Now: Hall of Fame, accessed September 10, 2012, http://www.invent.org/hall_of_fame/277.html.
16. Larry Mills, interview with author, July 17, 2012.
17. Dave Harris, interview by author, July 17, 2012.
18. Ibid.
19. Edward Craner, interview by author, July 17, 2012.
20. Ibid.

21. Ibid.

22. Harris interview.

Chapter 9

1. "Waldorf Salad," *Fawlty Towers*, BBC, March 5, 1979.

2. Craig Timberg, "Refugee from Facebook Questions the Social Media Life," *The Washington Post*, August 06, 2012, http://www.washingtonpost.com/business/economy/fugitive-from-facebook-questions-the-social-media-life/2012/08/03/5e4f855c-d0f3-11e1-adf2-d56eb210cdcd_story.html.

3. Tyler Thompson, "Redesigning the Boarding Pass—Journal—Boarding Pass/Fail," December 2009, http://passfail.squarespace.com/.

4. Dave Carroll, "United Breaks Guitars," performed by Dave Carroll and the Sons of Maxwell, YouTube.com, July 6, 2009, http://www.youtube.com/watch?v=5YGc4zOqozo.

5. Matt Fisher, "My Sister Paid Progressive Insurance to Defend Her Killer in Court," *Premium Fisher* (blog), August 13, 2012, http://mattfisher.tumblr.com/post/29338478278/my-sister-paid-progressive-insurance-to-defend-her.

6. Jay Baer and Amber Naslund, *The Now Revolution: 7 Shifts to Make Your Business Faster, Smarter, and More Social* (Hoboken, NJ: Wiley, 2011), xii.

7. Shelly Banjo, "Firms Take Online Reviews to Heart," *The Wall Street Journal*, July 30, 2012.

8. "What Is Big Data?—Bringing Big Data to the Enterprise," IBM corporate website, accessed March 4, 2012, http://www-01.ibm.com/software/data/bigdata/.

9. "TMT Predictions 2012, Billions and Billions: Big Data Becomes a Big Deal," Deloitte Consulting, January 17, 2012, http://www.deloitte.com/view/en_GX/global/industries/technology-media-telecommunications/tmt-predictions-2012/technology/70763e14447a4310VgnVCM1000001a56f00aRCRD.htm.

10. Paul Pellman, interview by author, June 15, 2012.

11. Doc Searls, *The Intention Economy: When Customers Take Charge* (Boston, MA: Harvard Business Review Press, 2012), 11.

12. Steve Patti, interview by author, August 8, 2012.

13. Peter Shankman, "The Greatest Customer Service Story Ever Told, Starring Morton's Steakhouse," Shankman.com, August 17, 2011, http://shankman.com/the-best-customer-service-story-ever-told-starring-mortons-steakhouse/.

14. Ibid.

15. Ibid.

16. Quirky | Social Product Development, accessed July 10, 2012, http://www.quirky.com/.

17. Jennifer Wang, "Quirky: The Solution to the Innovator's Dilemma," *Entrepreneur*, July 26, 2011, http://www.entrepreneur.com/article/220045.

18. Frank T. Piller, "Ten Reasons Why I Consider Quirky.com As Best in Crowdsourcing and Open Innovation," *Mass Customization & Open Innovation News*, October 14, 2010. http://mass-customization.de/2010/10/ten-reasons-why-i-consider-quirkycom-as-best-in-crowdsourcing-and-open-innovation.html.

19. Fiona Blades, online interview by author, August 22, 2012.

20. Emma K. Macdonald, Hugh N. Wilson, and Umut Konus, "Better Customer Insight—in Real Time," *Harvard Business Review* 90, no. 9 (September 2012): 103–108.

Chapter 10

1. Sheila Marikar, "American Airlines Fights Back After Alec Baldwin's Twitter Rant," ABC News, December 7, 2011, http://abcnews.go.com/blogs/entertainment/2011/12/alec-baldwin-what-happened-on-american-airlines-flight/.

2. Jason Hunter, telephone interview by author, August 11, 2011.

3. Steven Ellis, "Is André Rieu Bigger Than the Rolling Stones?" *The Austrailian*, November 1, 2008, http://www.theaustralian.com.au/arts/is-this-man-bigger-than-the-stones/story-e6frg8n6-1111117879188.

4. Mark Sutherland, "André Rieu Q&A," *Billboard*, May 7, 2010, http://www.billboard.com/features/andré-rieu-the-billboard-q-a-1004089453.story#/features/andré-rieu-the-billboard-q-a-1004089453.story.

5. Chrissey Iley, "André Rieu Interview," *The Telegraph*, March 30, 2011, http://www.telegraph.co.uk/culture/music/classicalmusic/8403549/Andre-Rieu-interview.html.

6. Ellis, "Is André Rieu Bigger Than the Rolling Stones?"

7. "2011 The Year in Music," *Billboard*, January 2012, http:/www.billboard.com/features/top-25-tours-of-2011-1005641362.story#/features/top-25-tours-of-2011-1005641362.story.

8. Pamela S. Leven, "Market Researchers Test Drive Products in Focus Groups, Where Honesty Is of Consuming Interest," *TWA Ambassador*, May 1998.

9. Brandon Gutman, "How Dos Equis Uses Facebook to Keep Its Man Interesting to Consumers," *Forbes*, February 9, 2012, http://www.forbes.com/sites/marketshare/2012/02/09/how-dos-equis-uses-facebook-to-keep-their-man-interesting-to-consumers/.

10. "Case Study Series: Dos Equis—A Triumph for Creative," *Bhatnaturally*, July 24, 2009, accessed September 10, 2012, www.bhatnaturally.com/advertising/dos-equis-campaign-case-study-a-triumph-for-creative.

11. "Introducing Dos Equis." Youtube.com. Accessed September 5, 2012.

12. EJ Schultz, "The Story Behind Dos Equis' Most Interesting Man in the World," *Creativity Online*, March 5, 2012, http://creativity-online.com/news/the-story-behind-dos-equis-most-interesting-man-in-the-world/233112.

13. Ibid.

14. Jeremy Mullman, "Dos Equis' 'Most Interesting Man' Is an Even Greater Beer Salesman, Euro's Gray-Bearded Creation for Heineken USA Import Has Led to Double-Digit Gains in Declining Category," *Ad Age*, July 15, 2009, http://adage.com/article/news/dos-equis-interesting-man-a-great-beer-salesman/137963/.

15. Chris Furnari, "The Hispanic Beer Equation," *BevNET*, July/August 2012, accessed August 3, 2012, http://www.brewbound.com/news/the-hispanic-beer-equation.

16. Clementine Fletcher, "Heineken Enlists Dos Equis to Win Back U.S. Drinkers: Retail," *Business Week*, December 20, 2011, http://www.businessweek.com/news/2011-12-20/heineken-enlists-dos-equis-to-win-back-u-s-drinkers-retail.html

17. Mullman, "Dos Equis' 'Most Interesting Man' Is an Even Greater Beer Salesman, Euro's Gray-Bearded Creation for Heineken USA Import Has Led to Double-Digit Gains in Declining Category,"

18. Dos Equis, The Most Interesting Man in The World, Facebook page, accessed September 7, 2012, http://www.facebook.com/pages/Dos-Equis-The-Most-Interesting-Man-In-The-World/177636282279658.

19. "The Most Interesting Academy," Dos Equis company website, accessed August 4, 2012, http://mostinterestingacademy.com/.

20. "Top Ten Fastest Growing Retailers, 2011," *Forbes*, April 4, 2011, accessed August 29, 2012.http://www.forbes.com/2011/04/11/amazon-apple-chipotle-netflix-business-fastest-growing-retailers_slide_6.html.

21. "Buffalo Wild Wings Investor Presentation, August 2012," Buffalo Wild Wings company website, accessed September 8, 2012, http://files.shareholder.com/downloads/BWLD/2030023393x0x504578/30DF4CE8-1D47-4E77-AC9A-B08EC00BFF43/08.30.2012_BWLD.pdf.

22. Elizabeth Olson, "Restaurants Reach Out to Customers with Social Media," *The New York Times*, January 19, 2011, http://www.nytimes.com/2011/01/20/business/media/20adco.html?_r=1.

23. Buffalo Wild Wings Facebook page, accessed September 7, 2012, http://www.facebook.com/BuffaloWildWings.

24. Anton Gonsalves, "Kentucky Manufacturer Big Ass Fans Turns a Commodity into a Brand," *Bloomberg*, June 8, 2011, http://www.bloom berg.com/news/2011-06-08/kentucky-manufacturer-big-ass-fans -turns-a-commodity-into-a-brand.html.

25. Jennifer Rooney, "Big Ass Fans Keeps Its Cool as It Moves Into Consumer Market," *Ad Age*, December 13, 2010, http://adage.com/article/ cmo-strategy/big-ass-fans-cool-moves-consumer-market/147647/.

26. Gonsalves, "Kentucky Manufacturer Big Ass Fans Turns a Commodity into a Brand."

27. Scott Sloan, "For Big Ass Fans CEO, Going against Grain Comes Naturally," Kentucky.com, June 3, 2012, http://www.kentucky .com/2012/06/03/2210446/for-big-ass-fans-ceo-going-against.html.

Chapter 11

1. John Mackey, "Conscious Capitalism: Creating a New Paradigm for Business," Whole Foods website, November 9, 2006, http://www2 .wholefoodsmarket.com/blogs/jmackey/2006/11/09/conscious-capitalism -creating-a-new-paradigm-for-business/.

2. John Paul DeJoria, "Paul Mitchell Co-Founder on Europe's Economic Crisis," interview by Neil Cavuto, *Cavuto*, FOX Business News, June 19, 2012,

3. Simon Mainwaring, *We First: How Brands and Consumers Use Social Media to Build a Better World*, (New York: Palgrave Macmillan, 2011), 47–48.

4. "Big Think Interview with Tony Hsieh: A Conversation with the CEO of Zappos," *Big Think*, October 11, 2010. http://bigthink.com/ideas/ 24384.

5. Mark Grurman, "Tim Cook Tells Apple Employees That Today's Victory Is About Values," *9to5Mac*, August 24, 2012, http://9to5mac.com/ 2012/08/24/tim-cook-tells-apple-employees-that-todays-victory-is-about -values/.

6. *The Treasure of the Sierra Madre*, directed by John Huston, Los Angeles, CA: Warner Bros. Pictures, 1948, DVD.

7. *TOMS Corporate Video*, TOMS company website, accessed June 2008, www.toms.com.

8. TOMS Shoes & Eyewear Company, accessed June 2012, http:// www.toms.com/.

9. Ibid.

10. Ibid.

11. Ibid.

12. Ibid.

13. *Toms Corporate Video*, TOMS company website, accessed June 2008, www.toms.com.

14. John R. Blackwell, "Luck Companies Brings Leadership Style to Region and Beyond," *Work It, Richmond*, April 15, 2012, http://workitrichmond.com/2012/04/15/luck-companies/.

15. Ibid.

16. Harry M. Jansen Kramer Jr., "The Only True Leadership Is Values-Based Leadership," *Forbes*, April 26, 2011, http://www.forbes.com/2011/04/26/values-based-leadership.html.

17. Blackwell, "Luck Companies Brings Leadership Style to Region and Beyond."

18. Luck Companies website, accessed August 29, 2012, http://luckcompanies.com/.

19. Ibid.

20. "Don't Buy This Jacket," Patagonia e-mail, November 28, 2011, http://www.patagonia.com/email/11/112811.html.

21. Yvon Chouinard and Nora Gallagher, "Don't Buy This Shirt Unless You Need It," Patagonia company website, Summer 2004, http://www.patagonia.com/us/patagonia.go?assetid=2388.

22. Seth Stevenson, "Patagonia's Founder Is America's Most Unlikely Business Guru," *The Wall Street Journal*, April 26, 2012, http://online.wsj.com/article/SB10001424052702303513404577352221465986612.html.

23. Ibid.

24. Yvon Chouinard, *Let My People Go Surfing: The Education of a Reluctant Businessman* (New York: Penguin Press, 2005), 21.

25. Monte Burke, "Wal-Mart, Patagonia Team to Green Business," *Forbes*, June 5, 2012, http://www.forbes.com/forbes/2010/0524/rebuilding-sustainability-eco-friendly-mr-green-jeans.html.

Chapter 12

1. Apple, "Think Different," advertisement, August 1997.

2. Daniel H. Pink, *A Whole New Mind: Moving from the Information Age to the Conceptual Age* (New York: Riverhead Books, 2005), 32.

3. Ibid.

4. Dr. Richard Lee, telephone interview by author, September 14, 2012.

ACKNOWLEDGMENTS

I think my initial attitude about writing yet another business book for an unsuspecting world was best expressed by the late, great comic genius Groucho Marx who said, "From the moment I picked your book up until I laid it down, I convulsed with laughter. Someday I intend on reading it." Fortunately, some serious people encouraged me to tell these stories in order to help other people along their business journeys. When writing a book, I learned you must surround yourself with family and friends that have the patience of Job. That's because as Abraham Lincoln said, "Books serve to a show a man that those original thoughts of his aren't very new after all." I bounced a lot of ideas off a lot of people about what you've read here and I was often humbled by their insistence on guiding me in a completely different direction. You talked and I listened. Now that I have completed the task at hand, I'd like to thank them.

Much, much gratitude to the three people who really believed in a new author from day one, my publishers extraordinaire, Erika Heilman and Jill Friedlander, co-founders of Bibliomotion and Rusty Shelton of Shelton Interactive. Thank you for your faith in me. Editor Susan Lauzau asked the right questions that made me think. Jill Schoenhaut kept the whole publishing process train running right on schedule. And many thanks to Susanna Kellogg and Emily Hanson for your persistence and patience. Thanks to Barbara Henricks of Cave Henricks Communications for your superb work and friendship. And thank you for the fantastic support from the entire Bibliomotion family of authors who have offered great support and encouragement.

Customer CEO has really been a family affair. For Franze, my wife and partner in every crazy adventure along the way, my love and thanks for helping me see that there was light at the end of the tunnel. To my dear mother Martha: you placed the love of reading in my heart and put the pen in my hand when you encouraged me to start writing so many years ago. That's a gift every mother should give their children. To my late father, "Big Chuck," thanks for the fine example of high character, endless courage, and the love of family you provided me. To son Chuck III, thanks for being my researcher and Devils Advocate through so much of this material. You made it a much better book than I could have ever done on my own. To son Alexander, thanks for bailing me out of so many tech-jams and always being my biggest encourager. To my sister Carolyn and her family Jerry, Jonathan, and Justin, thanks for your prayers and encouragement every step of the way.

So many friends, especially Michael Port, got the ball rolling for what became *Customer CEO*. Michael, you rock! Simon Mainwaring, you were an inspiration and great friend through this crazy (but good crazy) process. Thanks to all the contributors who shared their invaluable insight with me including Jason Hunter, Fiona Blades, Steve Patti, Paul Pellman, Landon Wood, Dave Harris, Edward Craner, Larry Mills, Elisa and Patrick Galloway, Tony TaCito, Dick Lee, Peter Shankman, and Marion Debruyne. And of course, Jason and Jennifer Smith, Bob Dugas, Elizabeth Darling, Danielle Behrens, Marie-Jeanne Juilland, Ed Schumacher, Tom Cuthbert, and Joseph Rodriguez. Thanks to my new friend Nate Ernsberger and the team at Compassion International for your help in creating the Water of Life partnership with my readers. Finally, thanks to my dear customers, who taught me the real value of listening. You've kept me on my toes for four decades and I owe you more than you'll ever know.

INDEX

Index

INDEX

Now that you've finished Customer CEO, isn't it time to profit from it?

Learn Much More About *Customer CEO.*

Let Chuck Wall lead you through a complete step-by-step program about today's customer. This executive education video series will fully equip you with even more tools, techniques and tips to profit from the power of your customers.

You can choose between our exclusive Customer CEO eLearning courses online or the complete executive education series on DVD, including comprehensive workbooks.

GET STARTED NOW AT
customerceoconsulting.com

Let Customer CEO Connect with Your Audience.

Get a fresh point of view about customers, innovation, marketing and the future of business with keynotes and workshops by author and entrepreneur Chuck Wall.

Chuck's messages and hands-on workshops will teach your executives, managers and employees how to really profit from the power of their customers.

Chuck is an expert in customer insight. His stories come from the real world of his long experience as an entrepreneur who has interviewed over 100,000 customers. He includes the newest research, tools, trends and tips so every company, no matter the size, can walk away enthused and fully engaged about the possibilities of more profitable and sustainable growth through better customer engagement.

Let Chuck help you design a better future for your business.

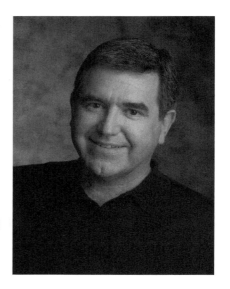

Plug In & Profit.
Listen to Customer CEO Podcasts with Chuck Wall.

Chuck interviews business and thought leaders about the lifeblood of every enterprise: the customer. Each episode features cutting edge thinking and solutions.

You will:

- Get the latest customer tips, trends and tools.

- Hear timely market research about what customers really want from companies today.

- Discover case studies about companies that are profiting from the power of their customers.

- Learn about customer-based marketing, storytelling and branding.

- Get answers to your questions.

Whether you are on the treadmill, in the car, or the office join the conversation at customerceoconsulting.com/podcasts.

CUSTOMER CEO™
Profit from the Power of Your Customers.
customerceoconsulting.com

Thank you for your support.

By buying this copy of *Customer CEO*, you have helped make a real difference in the life of a family in the developing world where fresh drinking water is a scarce resource.

Together, we are providing clean water to people in desperate need. Our partnership with Compassion International's Water of Life program means real action: one water system provides over a million gallons!

That's enough for a lifetime.

Read much more at customerceoconsulting.com/water.

And if you want to do more, Compassion would love to hear from you. You can contact them through our website.

Once again, thank you for your generosity.

0 1341 1571016 9

DATE DUE	RETURNED	